The Practical Guide to
Weekend
Parenting

The Practical Guide to
Weekend Parenting

101 Ways to Bond with Your Children While Having Fun

Doug Hewitt

healthyliving**books**

New York • London

Hatherleigh Press
5–22 46th Avenue, Suite 200
Long Island City, NY 11101
www.healthylivingbooks.com

Library of Congress Cataloging-in-Publication Data

Hewitt, Doug.
The practical guide to weekend parenting : 101 ways to bond with your children while having fun / Doug Hewitt.
    p. cm.
  ISBN-13: 978–1–57826–233–5
  1. Parenting, Part-time. 2. Parent and child. 3. Family recreation. 4. Creative activities
  and seat work. I. Title.
  HQ755.8.H484 2006
  649'.51—dc22

2006017880

ISBN-10: 1–57826–233-X
ISBN-13: 978–1–57826–233–5

Healthy Living Books are available for bulk purchase, special promotions, and premiums. For information on reselling and special purchase opportunities, please call us at 1-800-528-2550 and ask for the Special Sales Manager.

Cover design by Christine Weathersbee
Interior design by Deborah Miller

10 9 8 7 6 5 4 3 2
Printed in Canada

Acknowledgments

I would like to thank my mom and dad, June and Harve, who despite difficult times found time to do some weekend parenting on their own; the Writers Group of the Triad, based in Greensboro, North Carolina, for fostering a community of writers always eager to lend a helping hand; Alyssa, my editor, for her wonderful vision and skills; and Robin, proofreader extraordinaire, who provided unending help in the writing and shaping of this book.

Dedication

This is for Amy, who found the inner strength to circumnavigate the series of land mines known as high school to find and pursue her passion for teaching; for Andy, who discovered the courage to expand his horizons and confront the unknown in pursuit of excellence; for David, who has fine-tuned the ability to listen to his inner voice and has been unafraid to march to the beat of a different drummer; for Robin, who has against all odds persevered and found her way to make this world a much better place, and usually knows what I'm trying to say and puts it into words; for weekend parents everywhere, because they're the ones who put in the time and effort when satisfaction for a job well done is seldom acknowledged.

Contents

Introduction to Weekend Parenting

This book is for weekend parents, divorced, separated, or simply overwhelmed during the week, who need help in planning activities that will help their children grow into responsible adults. Even if you're not a parent, and are instead an aunt, uncle, or a child-care worker, you will find the advice useful. With your weekdays increasingly tied up with jobs, home maintenance, etc., it's difficult sometimes to plan effective activities on the weekend. This book will help.

Many of the activities in this book are geared for children thirteen and younger. Even so, some of the activities—such as kite flying—can be enjoyed by all. Teenagers might complain about being dragged out to fly a kite, but perhaps they'll understand that there is a child in each of us, no matter what age.

While its easiest to simply turn on the television set, if your children are to grow up to be the best they can be, they need to have other activities present in their lives. *The Practical Guide to Weekend Parenting* will help you actively participate with the raising, nurturing, and guidance of your children.

My children were two, three, and five when I was divorced. I made a decision to be involved with their lives and to be there for them. I wanted to see them every weekend, not every other weekend. Difficult? Yes. Costly? Absolutely. If you're a parent that wants to be there for your children, you can't see them only one day a month.

I've compiled 101 activities that worked for me, all designed to help your children grow into responsible adults. As you will notice as you go along, every chapter has tips and Parent-to-Parent Asides that might provide insights to everyone. Get ready for practical advice from the trenches from a parent who has been there and done that.

Have a low budget? Many of the activities are low cost or no cost. Are the children coming over for a week during the summer? Check the "Advance Planning Required" chapter.

Some chapters will not be helpful to everyone. I imagine the "Winter Activities" chapter will at first seem to be of little use to parents in Key West. But, hey, there are such things as vacations away from home.

Perhaps my favorite chapter is "Parenting from the Car Trunk". I say this because there are always little moments of time when you have ten minutes to kill. For example, you're dropping a child off at a friend's house, but the friend has been delayed and there's a ten-minute wait. Keeping activities in the trunk of your car offers you opportunities to use this time to make golden memories.

You might have to research some of the activities. For example one activity is Kites. You might need to visit the library. There are many books that explain kite building. The internet is another resource. Ask your friends. Have your children ask their friends. And if all else fails, try to build a kite on guesswork. Even if the kite fails to get airborne, you'll have helped your children by being a parent and sharing time with them.

Included with each activity is a While You're At It section where I list questions you can ask your children, topics to discuss, points to ponder aloud, etc. This is a book on practical parenting, and in a very practical way, it provides topics to discuss with your kids.

Family values means different things to different people. The premise of this book is simple: Doing activities with your children while having "open" conversations will give your children your own family values. You could talk for two hours straight while performing any one of these activities, but this isn't what will work. Asking questions, soliciting your children's input, conversing with your children while working/playing together on these activities will go a long way in helping your children grow up into mature, responsible adults.

So, browse by chapter, or read straight through. Then keep it for reference. If your children are old enough, let them read the book and suggest activities that appeal to them. This book, if it provides just a few ideas for parents trying to raise their kids on limited time and exposure, will be well worth the effort. Because there's no job more important, more difficult, and more rewarding than seeing your children grow into responsible, moral, ethical adults.

GUIDING PRINCIPLES

As a parent, I found that without guiding principles, many of the activities in this book might fall short of their potential to instill values in children.

PRINCIPLE 1

You have to "be there" for your kids. If you're a divorced parent, and you live a thousand miles away from your child, and your only communication is a letter during the holidays, then you're not an active parent. There's only so much that can be communicated over the telephone or by email. Most communication is by non-speech ways—body language. So, be there for your children. Be available on weekends, give rides to extracurricular activities if asked, make phone calls during the week. If you're in the process of getting a divorce or are separating, it's important to stay geographically close to your kids.

PRINCIPLE 2

You have to listen to your children. Really listen. Sometimes they don't know the words to express their thoughts and feelings. They are flooded with new situations every day. They are learning to cope. Don't blow them off with a "This too shall pass" or "Have faith" or "Say a prayer" at every turn. You might not have an answer for every question, but saying "I've wondered how to handle that, too" would help your child understand that sometimes answers are difficult to come by. Offer some options. Think out loud. I've found that while I'm tossing out ideas, my children will often think of an option by themselves. Sometimes they just don't know how to "think out loud" and you can help them discover this talent.

PRINCIPLE 3

You have to allow your children to make decisions. This goes, in part, with Principle 2. Ask your kids for input, then listen. Let them make the call on where to go on a Saturday afternoon. Let them make mistakes (that is, as long as safety isn't compromised, such as deciding to see how a lighted match affects a gas can). If they want to build a model car without reading the directions, let them. One of my sons when in the fourth grade surprised me by succeeding at this. It never worked for me. I always had leftover parts (darn those camshafts!).

PRINCIPLE 4

Tell your kids you're proud of them from time to time. They might sense this, but if you never say it, will they ever know for certain? When they do a good job, tell them you've noticed. When they don't, tell them you're proud they tried.

PRINCIPLE 5

Every child is different. What works for one might not work for another. You might, with one of your children, only have to read a fable to teach a moral lesson. With another child, you might have to draw upon real-life experiences to teach the same lesson. One of my children loves basketball. Another likes chess and dislikes all sports. My third child is dedicated to the performing arts. Urge each of your children to pursue their individual interests.

PRINCIPLE 6

Apologize to your kids when you're wrong. If you think you're never wrong, you may need to confront this before you continue reading this book. If you think your kids don't know when you screw up, you're forgetting some of your observations during your own childhood.

PRINCIPLE 7

Explain yourself to your children. I cringe when I hear a parent tell a child they should do something "because I say so." This teaches children they don't have to justify their actions to anyone. It short-circuits reason. If having no explanation is good enough for a parent, it'll be good enough for the child who is entering adulthood.

PRINCIPLE 8

Remember that raising children is tough. There's no single right way to raise a child successfully, and in fact no single way to define what a successful child-rearing experience is. And so there'll be times when things don't go right. Hang in there. Life has a way of balancing out.

PRINCIPLE 9

Don't fall into the martyr syndrome trap. Don't say, "I've given my whole life to you and this is what I get?" Try not to lay guilt trips on your children. Often they feel responsible enough for all of the woes around them. There's no need to pile it on. And of course, as a parent, you have to give up some things. You can't go cavorting off to Timbuktu every other year, but don't hold this against your kids. This should be your choice, not theirs.

PRINCIPLE 10

Be honest with your kids. Don't make them do things out of guilt. Don't constantly play tricks on them. They'll learn not to trust you. Don't tease them excessively. This will sow confusion. Think "moderation." Some joking around can teach a child a sense of humor. Too much can make them feel like the butt of a cosmic joke, that the world is laughing at them. And when you use humor, show them you can laugh at yourself.

PRINCIPLE 11

Play with your kids. Children learn the rules of society through play. They learn a sense of what's fair. Plus, it's a good way to bond. Let them laugh. Let them not take something seriously, such as the outcome of a game. If your child never laughs, wouldn't that be a shame? When children learn to play, they learn to be creative. They learn how to use their minds.

PRINCIPLE 12

Don't use the "Do as I say, not as I do" line. It's stupid, insulting, doesn't work, and it teaches that you live your life with a double standard.

CHAPTER 1

At Home

● ●

If you're a homebody like me, you'll enjoy the activities in this chapter. There's no need to step outside. But even if you're an outdoors person, or you like to travel, there will be times when you need activities to do inside your house. Home is where the heart is, they say, and so the activities in this chapter will help your children think of your house as their home.

AT HOME ACTIVITIES
Mural Painting

Board Games

Card Games

Letter Writing

Marble Games

Draw Pictures

Carve Soap

Shape Clay

MURAL PAINTING

This can be done on an out-of-the-way wall, the inside of a closet, or the back of a closet door. Talk it over with your children. What kind of theme do they want? A garden theme? How about science (starscape or a distant planet)? An underwater theme?

You should draw the mural on paper first, then outline the design in pencil on the wall. Then fill in the lines with paint. If you live in an apartment (or in a house and aren't brave enough), cover the wall with poster board first.

This project can be done in several ways. You can give each child a different part of the wall, or have everyone work on the entire wall. Should you try to make this look as realistic as possible, or maybe something a bit more impressionistic? Talk it over with your kids. Have them vote on it. It's their mural!

PARENT-TO-PARENT ASIDE

Although it's important to keep control of whatever situation I'm in with my children, they need to learn to have control of their own lives. It's a part of growing up. Having them vote on things is a great way to do this. Of course, I've tried to sway many such votes, but the interesting thing is that sometimes when my children voted in a way different that I would've voted, they were proven right. And this is a great time to point out such a thing. You should try to let children know early that you're not perfect. Otherwise, when they get to be teenagers and figure it out for themselves, they tend to rebel to prove their point.

WHILE YOU'RE PAINTING YOUR MURAL:

* What are their favorite colors? Any idea why?
* Why is red considered a warm color and dark blue a cold color? (Talk about the rainbow and its colors.)
* What colors can be mixed to produce green? (Yellow and blue.) What other colors can be mixed?

* What animals use color to hide from other animals, to blend in with their habitat? (A chameleon.)

* How can a mural, or a single picture, seem to tell a whole story? (Our imagination gives us clues to explain what we see.)

* Why is it said that a picture is worth a thousand words? (A single picture can show us many things that can take a lot of words to describe.)

BOARD GAMES

There are dozens of board games that children enjoy playing. And it doesn't matter who wins! This provides excellent time to talk to your children. Of course, consider the age of your children when selecting a board game to play. Try checkers for younger kids, then move on to chess as they grow older. But no matter what the age, board games not only provide you with a chance to grow closer to your children, they can be instructional. Monopoly, for example, can help with lessons about money. Chess and checkers teach strategy. Trivial Pursuit might not be ideal for younger children, but it's a great game to learn fun facts. Games like Clue can help deductive reasoning. A great game to help kids learn new words, and how to spell them, is Scrabble.

PARENT-TO-PARENT ASIDE

While the best board games allow for more than two players, it's good to have games for one-on-one play too, like Battleship or checkers (especially if you have only one child). It's good for the children to all play together. There will be the usual bickering, the "you're taking too long to roll the dice!" admonishments, and as a parent you should always try to maintain a voice of reason. "Maybe he took a long time because he/she was strategizing," I might suggest. Use humor, or play the role of the dumb cop. "Hey, I'm just trying to get along," you might say.

If you have more than one child, it's good also to play the game in a round-robin; that is, you play against each child one at a time. This will help give each child the one-on-one attention that every child (and every adult!) needs from time to time.

WHILE YOU'RE PLAYING BOARD GAMES:

* What does "having a strategy" mean? (Planning your moves in advance.)

* Talk about winning versus losing. For example, there are, in any particular pro sport, many teams but only one that wins the championship. Does that make the pro players on the other teams losers?

* In the long run, is losing a game important? Why or why not?

CARD GAMES

Many of the same parenting techniques can be used in card games that you used when playing board games. Card games have one huge advantage, though. They're extremely portable and can easily be taken on road trips. There's nothing wrong when taking your child to the dentist's office and during the obligatory long-term wait taking out a deck of cards and starting a quick game of Go Fish. Some games for younger players are Crazy 8's and Old Maid.

Cards aren't limited to only gaming, either. Why not pick up a book on magic tricks, pull out your card deck, and amaze your kids with your mind-reading?

PARENT-TO-PARENT ASIDE

There are hundreds of opportunities to interact with your children while you are waiting near your car. Maybe you've gone to see a parade but it got cancelled, or perhaps you arrived early. Having a "trunk kit" for activities to do with your children during those unexpected free periods of time is great for the practical parent. A deck of cards is great for this kit. See the chapter titled "Parenting from the Car Trunk".

WHILE YOU'RE PLAYING CARDS:

* Ask your children how their week went.
* Did they make any new friends?
* How do they like their teachers?
* Ask them to describe in detail one of their days, and ask questions if they aren't specific enough.
* What's a suit? How many cards are in each suit? (A suit is a set of cards with the same group designation. In a standard deck, the four suits are hearts, clubs, diamonds, and spades. Thirteen cards in each suit for a total of 52.)
* In which direction are cards dealt? (In North America, clockwise, but there are places in the worlds where cards are dealt counterclockwise.)

LETTER WRITING

Encourage your children to write letters to their friends. The world of emails is taking over, and giving your children an ability to write letters will help them later in life. Have them write to relatives who don't live nearby. It's important to stay in touch with far-away relatives. As the saying goes, blood is thicker than water, and you can explain the meaning of this to your kids. As likely as not, your children will complain that they won't know what to say. Have them describe their past week. What were the highlights? The low points? They can also send an idea to a politician on a current event. What do they think is unfair in the world? They could write a letter to a congressman and suggest they support, for example, laws for reduced pollution. You can also suggest that your children find a pen pal through organizations such as Kids' Media Club. Schoolteachers can help find pen pals, too.

Wouldn't it be great to get a letter from the President? Try writing a letter and see. Send it to: The White House, 1600 Pennsylvania Avenue NW, Washington, DC 20500.

PARENT-TO-PARENT ASIDE

Congressmen, or their aides, will always respond to letters, so it helps children to see that their voices are heard. The topic of their letters can also provide topics for conversation later. For example, the next time a law that concerns pollution is passed, you can talk with your child about how he/she had a say in it. On the other hand, writing a poem or a short story is a wonderful way to fire those synopses in a child's creative part of the brain. Usually, during the course of a school year, there are poetry or story competitions that a child can enter. Keep copies! You can give them to your children when they're grown up and the both of you can have another moment of bonding.

WHILE YOU'RE WRITING POEMS AND CORRESPONDENCE:

* How does the U.S. Postal Service work? What about air mail? (Letters going via air mail go by plane, which is especially quicker when sending overseas.)

* How do they feel when they get a birthday card?

* What's the best letter they ever got?

* What's the best letter they can imagine getting? What's the best letter they can imagine sending?

* Who in the world is in the most need of a supportive letter? Soldiers overseas? The President?

MARBLE GAMES

This is a low-cost activity that can be hours of fun. There are books on this subject (check library), but you can design your own games. For example, get a shoebox and cut different size holes in it. Have a contest to see who can roll a marble through the hole. The winner wins free marbles. And the smaller the hole, the greater the number of marbles. Have each child design a unique contest. Take guesses as to how many marbles will fill a jar. See who's closest.

Here are three basic marble games.

Ringer. With a piece of chalk, draw a circle on your driveway 10 feet across. Make an "X" with thirteen marbles in the middle of the circle. Take turns, from anywhere outside the circle, shooting a marble at the marbles inside the circle. Any marble knocked outside the circle counts as one point. If your marble doesn't make it outside the circle, it stays!

Bull's Eye. Draw a circle 1 foot across. Draw a circle outside the first circle, leaving a foot between the lines. Continue this for 5 circles. From a distance of 10 feet from the outer circle, try shooting marbles for the center circle. A marble in the center circle counts as 5 points, the second circle 4 points, etc. Shoot 10 marbles and see who has the high score.

Marble Golf. This is played like normal golf, except you might have to select targets instead of holes. If you have a yard, you could dig small holes.

PARENT-TO-PARENT ASIDE

When I started projects such as these marble games, I found that it provided a wonderful chance for my children to bring their friends into the mix. Not only could my children invite their friends over and participate in these marble contest marathons, my kids could use this marble contest platform as a way to provide interesting conversation at school. It could help them make friends, and making friends can be very difficult for children. Often it seems daunting to them—far more than we as parents remember it being.

While You're Playing with Marbles:

* Are dice nothing more than square marbles? Why or why not? (A marble is a little ball, and if it's square, it's not a ball.)

* Why do you tend to slip and fall if you step on a marble? (Marbles act like ball bearings, and just like a car wheel uses ball bearings to turn without resistance, you can slip and fall.)

* What's the difference between a marble and a round seed? Why won't a marble grow when planted? (Marbles are made of lifeless materials, such as glass, and cannot grow, while seeds come from living organisms and are designed to grow into new living organisms.)

* Ask your children if they're interested in organizing a "Marble Olympics" with their friends. You can make ribbons for "medals" and hand out awards for 1st, 2nd, and 3rd for each game.

DRAW PICTURES

FUN FACT
Some cavemen drew pictures of animals on the walls of their caves as long ago as the Ice Age.

Devote an afternoon to drawing. If they are getting bored with one type of drawing, try providing different materials. Use color pencils, felt tip pens, or water colors. Framing a child's artwork and placing it on the wall is an excellent way to promote a child's self-esteem. I suggest placing the artwork where it can be updated periodically. Save the old pictures. Teenagers will look back with amusement at their kindergarten drawings.

PARENT-TO-PARENT ASIDE

I still have artwork I made in the seventh grade. Somehow it helps me feel like I understand the continuity of my life. I don't save every piece of artwork my children bring home from school, but I do have a cabinet into which I put pieces I believe are representative of their age and talent. Some day they'll appreciate it when I present them with an album of their artwork through the years. It's always good to remind your children that "beauty is in the eye of the beholder" and that "one man's trash is another man's treasure."

WHILE YOU'RE DRAWING:

* Ask if people have different tastes as to what is considered "good art."

* What does "symbol" mean? If you draw a stick-man, how is it that everyone knows what it represents?

* What does creating a piece of art mean? Is it "art" because it's something that never existed before? How does it feel to make something new?

CARVE SOAP

Provide your kids with a bar of regular, white bath soap and let their imaginations run free. Please use common sense with carving and give them blunt objects (such as spoons) to carve the soap. If your children don't know what to carve, try browsing a magazine for ideas.

PARENT-TO-PARENT ASIDE

It's a good idea to have a knickknack shelf somewhere in your house. If you go on a trip somewhere, buy a souvenir and put it on the knickknack shelf as a reminder of the time you spent with your children. I like to put some of the soap carvings on the knickknack shelf. I consider it a display of the "growing together" of my children and me.

WHILE YOU'RE SOAP CARVING:

* What's the difference between 3-dimensional art (statues, for example) and 2-dimensional art (a painting)?

* What's better, carving or painting? Is it a personal preference?

* Is it possible to carve out a felled tree to make a canoe? Is that what American Indians did? What are some ways they did this? (They burned a hole in the tree to make it easier to carve.)

* What are some of the practical things made with carving? (Frames for pictures? Golf tees? Candy bowls? Tent pegs?)

> **FUN FACT**
> *Art can be 3D. Gargoyles on castles and churches were once designed to scare away bad demons from entering, but they had a dual-use as rain-spouts.*

SHAPE CLAY

From Play-Doh to Sculpey, molding clay is a great way to help children learn how to use their hands. It helps the child develop the sense of being able to mold into reality the images they have in their heads. Brag about the results (and exhibit them) to people who come to visit. If your children need ideas for what to make with their clay, look through magazines, talk about TV shows or maybe just look out the window.

PARENT-TO-PARENT ASIDE

Sometimes it's best to bite your tongue. For example, I've always tried to guide my children into activities that would help them later in life. My daughter is very tall, and I encouraged her to play basketball, first in the community leagues, then later at her middle and high schools. Throughout the years, I always supported her and praised her performance and effort.

When she decided in the tenth grade to not play anymore because she wanted to devote her time to the marching band and school plays, I told her that it was her decision and her life and I would support whatever she decided, even though I believed she was good enough to earn a college basketball scholarship. She later told me that was the moment she realized just how "great" a dad I was, because she knew that deep-down I wanted to her to play basketball. She said that moment inspired her to have faith in herself.

WHILE YOU'RE MODELING CLAY:

* How is carving soap different than modeling clay? Can the same item be made either way? What if a mistake is made while carving? Is it correctable?

* What does a kiln do? Does setting clay out in the sun do the same thing?

* Is there anything around the house that looks like it was made by using clay?

* Is it better to make something practical with clay or something that's just nice to look at?

THE PRACTICAL GUIDE TO WEEKEND PARENTING

CHAPTER 2

In the Yard

• •

The activities in this chapter are designed for outdoor fun, and you need to go no farther than your own backyard. Your yard can provide hours of fun and entertainment.

There's no substitute for nature, no matter how realistic those video games are becoming. Getting outside automatically gets the TV turned off. What a great thing! Some kids would rather watch television when you come up with the suggestion, "Let's go outside!" "And do what?" they might ask. Well, here you have a handy list of activities to do in your yard. Try one a month. After a few activities, they might even start prompting you to go outdoors! Ask them to come up with their own yard activities. If they have neighborhood friends, you can have your children invite them over to join in on the fun.

I have discovered that outdoor activities helped my children burn excess energy. Whenever I took my kids outside, I never had a problem in getting them to sleep that night.

> **IN THE YARD ACTIVITIES**
> Plant a Garden
> Roast Marshmallows
> Fort Building
> Catch Lightning Bugs
> Construct Mechanical Gardens
> Search for Four-Leaf Clovers

PLANT A GARDEN

If you have a green thumb, this may be a fun way to pass it on to your kids, and get them outdoors. Don't make this more complicated than it needs to be! You can get seedlings from people who already have plants, or pick up seed packets from most stores, including your local grocery store. The outdoor space you have will determine how much "room" to give to your kids. If you have a yard, give each child a plot to work with. If you live in an apartment, give each a window sill. Plan your garden in advance on graph paper. You could do some preparing by visiting a nursery to see what kind of plants your children might be interested in growing. For the very young, I suggest trying sunflowers, zinnias, or beans. These sprout quickly and grow very fast. Take "before and after" pictures and put them in your scrapbook.

PARENT-TO-PARENT ASIDE

When my children grew plants, topics for conversation grew with them. For example, the question that was asked over and over again for me was: How do seeds know what to grow up into? Before science explained genetics, this was not an easy question. You'll find that kids are savvier these days, having seen *Jurassic Park* and other movies.

Talking about a plant's life cycle can also raise perhaps one of the most difficult subjects to deal with—death. I remember the moment as a child when I realized I would someday die. Talk about a downer! I cried and cried, and I know I didn't have anyone to talk to about my feelings and my questions. I've talked to my children about the subject, of course, and this is one of the times where your own views should be shared with your child to make this less frightening. My daughter asked me what we will look like in the afterlife and, after admitting that I can't say for sure, having not been actually dead, I replied that we will look like how we picture ourselves. It's just one reason that we need to try to be the best people we can be, and to understand what "best" means.

WHILE YOU'RE PLANTING SEEDS AND SEEDLINGS:

* How do plants grow? (Plants grow much like people! They eat! Their roots absorb minerals and water, and their leaves take in sunlight.)

* Why do living things seem to do better when they're cared for? (Like people, plants need things to be healthy. Neglected plants might not get enough water or sunlight, and they'll wither as a result. Being a caregiver means giving a plant what it needs to grow.)

* Would they prefer a colorful flower or a food-producing plant like a tomato plant?

* What are some of the differences between a plant that grows in the desert (cactus) and one that grows near a pond (water lily)? (A cactus has a waxy skin to help keep in water it collects. Its needles not only provide shade for the cactus, the needles discourage animals from trying to eat it. Now that's a mouthful! A water lily has leaves that are large and light to help it float on the water and to lie flat on the water surface so that it can collect as much sunlight as possible, which is not an issue in the desert! It makes a great resting spot for frogs!)

* Talk about the four seasons and how plants and trees react to them where you live.

* See who can name the most plants that are edible.

ROAST MARSHMALLOWS

Here's an outdoor activity that requires just a bit of prep work. Buy graham crackers and chocolate bars and marshmallows. Your object here is to layer the chocolate on the crackers, then coat the chocolate with gooey marshmallow. You'll need to build a small campfire in the backyard, or use a small Hibachi grill. You could purchase cans of Sterno cooking fuel for an even safer alternative.

Find some sticks and sharpen the ends, peeling off the bark. Now, spike the marshmallow on your stick and toast carefully over the flame. You should monitor your children carefully so they do not set more on fire than just the candy!

Every child should have a graham cracker and a candy bar, broken into two pieces with the chocolate on top. Once you've melted your marshmallow, put it on your chocolate-stacked cracker, and top with the second chocolate and cracker. Enjoy!

PARENT-TO-PARENT ASIDE

If you're a weekend parent, you might not have safety on the top of your list of mental activities when the kids come over. But when safety is involved, you don't get a second chance. It only takes one screw-up to cause serious injury. There're no do-overs. Talk to your children about fire safety. What can catch fire in the house? Are fires ever allowed to be unattended? How do you make sure the fire is out when you're finished? Talk about the number of people killed in house fires in the U.S. every year. In recent years, the average number of deaths in the U.S. from house fires is over 3,000 annually. This is a good time to also talk about a fire plan (including evacuation routes, crawling below smoke, an outside meeting location, etc.), and if you don't have one, you need to get one right away.

WHILE YOU'RE ROASTING MARSHMALLOWS:

* Does anyone know of a house that burned down? Has any been in the news lately?

* What other kinds of cracker combinations can you make in the future? What would it take to start making and selling them? What would happen if you sold some and people got sick? (Lawsuit!)

* What does the term "breaking bread together" mean? (In the days before silverware such as forks and knives, loaves of bread were literally broken apart by hand in order to eat. Although we cut our bread now with knives, or get it sliced from the grocery store, "breaking bread" still refers to eating a meal.)

* Why does having a meal together strengthen the bonds between people? (It's a ritual that helps families stay bonded.)

* What does "stop, drop, and roll" mean? (If your clothes catch fire, running will fan the flames. Stopping and rolling back and forth on the ground can help put out flames.)

FORT BUILDING

Playtime can be quite simple. To build your child's fort, try throwing a sheet or a blanket over a table. Instant fort, and instant privacy! Maybe you can find a large cardboard box. If you have multiple children, try giving them each a fort, and maybe hook up an intercom system with two empty tin cans connected by a piece of string. If they are higher-tech and have walkie-talkies, use them. Do your parent-check and be sure that the forts are not closed off to the point where there is no fresh air. Kids need to breathe, fort or no fort.

PARENT-TO-PARENT ASIDE

One of the neat things about forts is that it will give your children a sense of ownership and privacy. They'll never mature as adults unless they learn to operate outside of your sphere of influence. A child needs to be able to (eventually) have secrets, or at least things they don't necessarily need to tell their parents. A fort (or clubhouse, perhaps, for the daughters) is a good start.

WHILE YOU'RE MAKING A FORT:

* What are some of the favorite forts in history? What about the Alamo? What makes it so special? (Although Jim Bowie of bowie knife fame and Davy Crockett died at the Alamo while defending it from Mexican forces, "Remember the Alamo" became a successful rallying cry for Texan independence from Mexico.)

* Are castles a kind of fort? (Yes, because they are a kind of "fortification.")

* Were there a lot of forts in America during the days of the Wild West? (There were many military outposts, but they were too widely scattered to prevent the West from being Wild.)

* Talk about Fort Knox. (Fort Knox stores over 5,000 tons of gold! During World War II, Fort Knox protected the Declaration of Independence and the U.S. Constitution.)

CATCH LIGHTNING BUGS

On a warm summer night the fireflies come out. If you have a big backyard, they are probably everywhere! For this activity, you'll need a large jar (like the ones used for canning). Have your children run around catching lightning bugs and bringing them back to you to place them in the jar (make sure there are air holes in the lid). The next evening, after a long night, show your child how to respect nature by releasing them back outside.

PARENT-TO-PARENT ASIDE

Sometimes, when I give my kids an activity to do, I stand back and watch after saying, "Go forth and catch bugs!" Staying back helped develop their sense of independence. On the other hand, sometimes I would join in. "I want to catch bugs, too!" Joining in helped strengthen the bond between us. So, try it each way and see which works best with your children. Try alternating methods.

WHILE YOU'RE CATCHING LIGHTNING BUGS:

* Explain how the light is produced by a chemical reaction. (The lightning bug mixes two chemicals in its abdomen along with oxygen from an air tube. By controlling the amount of oxygen, the lightning bug can control the brightness of the light.)

* Talk about sea creatures that can produce light. (Lantern-eye fish, cookie cutter shark, flashlight fish, angler fish, gulper eel. The angler fish "angles" or fishes for its meal with a glowing worm-like appendage.)

* What other ways are there to produce light? (Fire, electricity, etc.)

* What do the bugs use the light for? (Mating.)

FUN FACT:
There is one species of firefly whose females flash in many different ways to attract other species males. When the wrong species male arrives, he is eaten.

CONSTRUCT MECHANICAL GARDENS

If it's the middle of winter, or you are thinking of something a bit more eternal to put in your windowsill, you may want to think about creating a mechanical garden. Take a trip to a hobby shop for this, and think about what you can make with pipe cleaners and colored ribbons. Some other items you can use are Popsicle sticks, different colored cloth, plastic drink bottles, foam rubber, straws, and plastic cups. Create some fake flowers and put them in a vase that you make from a plastic cup filled with marbles or stones. You could even fashion some butterflies by cutting out wings from colored paper and glue them together. Attach the butterfly to a pipe cleaner and place it so that the butterfly appears to have been attracted to your flowers. And hey, you won't ever have to water these plants!

PARENT-TO-PARENT ASIDE

Talk about the importance of recycling, which not only helps the planet, it saves you money! You can give them a first-hand lesson when creating a mechanical garden by using recycled materials that otherwise would be heading for the trash. Empty toothpaste tubes, cardboard tubes from empty toilet paper rolls, colorful packaging material from food bought at the grocery store, such as potato chip bags. Bottle caps come in a wide variety of colors and can be glued together to create flower petals.

WHILE YOU'RE MAKING A MECHANICAL GARDEN:

* See if you can fashion different flowers with different "personalities". Maybe some of your flowers are strong, some lanky, some shy.

* Given unlimited resources, what kind of mechanical garden would your children construct? How big a flower could you make with a rocket from NASA? (Astronomically big!)

* Think of names for your mechanical gardens. (Such as the Rose Garden at the White House. How about Marvin Gardens? Pleasant Garden?)

* Think about inviting friends and family over for a garden tour.

THE PRACTICAL GUIDE TO WEEKEND PARENTING

SEARCH FOR FOUR-LEAF CLOVERS

If it's a sunny afternoon and you're looking for a low-key activity to occupy a lot of time—and patience—sit down in a field of clover and start searching for four-leaf clovers. You can make it into a game: Who can find one first? How many can you find in half an hour? Can you find clovers that are different shades of green? Maybe you can look for other unusual plants, or colorful plants. Everybody can talk about their search technique. Do they look at each clover, one at a time? Or maybe they have a wider focus and look for something that doesn't match like in those "what doesn't belong" drawings.

When you get home be sure to preserve your four-leaf clover for posterity. You can do this by setting an iron on light heat and pressing the clover between sheets of wax paper, or placing it inside a very heavy book, such as a dictionary.

PARENT-TO-PARENT ASIDE

Four-leaf clovers stand out from their three-leaf kin because they're different. In a world in which many, if not most, children are trying to "fit in," there are times when it's good to stand apart from the crowd: Getting a high test score; excelling in athletics; being creatively unique in one of the performing arts. So, while it's natural to want to fit in, talk to your kids about the advantages of being unique, from having a stand-out resume when job hunting, to the self-satisfaction of having their own identity.

WHILE YOU'RE LOOKING FOR FOUR-LEAF CLOVERS:

* Ask your children if they believe in "luck." Do people make their own luck? (Many people think so.)
* Are there such things as five-leaf clovers? (Yes.)
* Where does the term "what goes around, comes around" mean? (No, it doesn't refer to a Merry-Go-Round; it refers to karma and how the way you treat other people will be, sooner or later, the way you will be treated.)
* What about "the luck of the Irish?" (Some people believe this refers to how the Irish must have had good luck to overcome great adversity such as the potato famine. And, of course, the shamrock is a symbol of Ireland.)

> **FUN FACT:**
> On average, there are 10,000 three-leaf clovers for every instance of a true four-leaf clover.

CHAPTER 3

At the Park

It's nice to go outside and do activities in your yard. But maybe you need a larger space. Maybe you want to throw a Frisbee as far as you can, and your yard just isn't big enough. There's a solution—head out for the park! There's another advantage to going to the park, and lucky you if you have a park in walking distance. But I know some parents who have sizeable yards, and their children go outside often and play, but there's seldom anyone else around. Going to the park helps your children understand that there are other children like them out there in the world, and they like to play, too! Of course, they meet children in school, but that's different. That's school.

The activities in this chapter are designed for you and your children to grow together, to learn, and to have fun at the same time.

> ## AT THE PARK ACTIVITIES
> Kites
> Paper Airplanes
> Puddle Splashing
> Picnics
> Playground

KITES

Flying a kite is more fun if you make it yourself. Talk this project over with your children and draw up some plans (perhaps browsing the Internet for ideas). I suggest starting with the basic diamond shape typically seen in stores in spring. When you are ready, make a list of the supplies you need, then go hunt for them in-house or shop for them at a mall.

Prompt your children to be creative, perhaps by naming their kites and painting the name on it, such as *Skymaster* or *Sails On Wind*. Naming the kite for a pet or a person in the news might be fun. Of course, depending on what the latest craze is, names such as *Pikachu* and *Nemo* may be appropriate.

If your child is more ambitious, try building a box kite. You might have to go on a field trip to the library to find designs, but this can be fun in itself and teaches children how to use resources to find the information they need. More and more, we live in an information age, and it doesn't hurt to get children thinking about how to locate that information, and then how to use it.

You'll have to find an open field to try out your creations. Remember that Charlie Brown, no matter how hard he tried, managed to find the kite-eating tree. Bring snacks and make an afternoon of it. Award ribbons or prizes for the kite that stays up the longest, the most colorful, the biggest, the smallest, etc. Make sure that each child gets at least one prize.

PARENT-TO-PARENT ASIDE

I've found that it's always worked out best when my children each receive the same number of prizes, the same number of holiday presents, etc. I've broken up packs of three in order to give a child two of something. What's proven interesting is that my kids have caught on to this and have come to understand that it's just Dad's way of trying to be fair, even when they understand that a good, expensive present is worth more than ten cheap gifts from the dollar store. They roll their eyes a bit, but they understand how important they must be to me if I'm going through such excruciating mathematical calculations.

WHILE YOU'RE BUILDING YOUR KITE:

* Ask your children if they've thought about being a pilot.

* What's it like to be a bird? An astronaut?

* Have they ever dreamed they were flying? Have you?

* Why did Ben Franklin fly a kite? (He discovered electricity with a key. When discussing this, also describe how dangerous this is.)

* How many people thought the Wright Brothers were crazy? (Everyone!)

* How do clouds stay up in the sky? (They are lighter than the air.)

PAPER AIRPLANES

There are lots of books on making paper airplanes, and some ideas can be found on the internet. Don't have internet access? Many libraries do. Call and check. After you make the planes, have a "Flight Competition" with awards to longest distance flight, most air time, and best aesthetic design. You can have each child build three different paper airplanes, using different construction techniques, "testing" them to see what works best. You can use different thicknesses of paper. Try putting tape on the edges of your wings. Maybe the strategic placement of paper clips near the front of your plane will help. Folding up the back edges of your wings can also change the flight dynamics of your plane. Ask your children if they have a science teacher who might be interested in giving out extra credit for a report of paper airplane flight dynamics!

PARENT-TO-PARENT ASIDE

As I have mentioned before, if you have more than one child, it's always a good idea to have each child win in at least one category. And if you have to make up a category, such as "Best Flight by Youngest Member in Family," then do so.

Some of the questions I suggest have difficult answers. For example, in the following list, I suggest asking, "Why is it so difficult to predict the weather?" There may be no easy answer to this question. Have your kids ask local teachers or meteorologists at a local TV station. Remember that philosophical answers are fun, too, such as: "Because wouldn't life get boring if we could predict everything." or "It's a plot by manufacturers to sell umbrellas."

WHILE YOU'RE MAKING PAPER AIRPLANES:

* What does "air current" mean? (Just like you can see water moving in a river current, there are movements of air in "currents.")
* Are weather forecasters always right? (No!)

* Why is it so difficult to predict the weather? (It's not too difficult to predict the weather five minutes from now, but what about five days? It's difficult because there are too many variables!)

* What are some of the differences between airplanes and kites? (Kites have no wings and require wind, while airplanes and gliders do not need wind and they have wings that help them create "lift.")

* Which would they prefer, longer flights or higher flights?

PUDDLE SPLASHING

Every kid needs to splash through a puddle at least once in their life. Make sure you do this only if it's a warm rain—and there's no hint of lightning or thunder. Always make sure everyone is dry before going back inside. Remove wet, muddy shoes at the door so the mud isn't tracked through the house.

Isn't it great to walk barefoot through the park and get mud oozing between your toes? I suggest washing the mud off of any clothes before dropping your kids off with the weekday parent, allowing you to claim some degree of responsibility. If puddle-jumping seems a bit out of your league, remember that a short walk in the rain is nice, too.

PARENT-TO-PARENT ASIDE

Splashing through puddles is great fun, but as a weekend parent you have a responsibility for your children that goes beyond having fun. Make sure at some point that you discuss responsibility with the other "weekday" parent and teach your children that they respect both parents, as many children pick up on hidden (or not so hidden) agendas.

WHILE YOU'RE OUT IN THE RAIN:

* Where does the saying about "I won't melt" come from? (It means that you're not made of sugar, and of course sugar implies sweetness.)

* Does sugar melt when it gets wet? (It actually dissolves.) Does that make you and your children not sweet? (No!)

* How does water get up in the sky? If water evaporates, does that mean that there's water vapor all around in the air? Does that mean that there are things all around us that exist but that we can't see? (Yes! Wind, microbes, and electronics transmissions from radio, TV, and cell phones are all examples.)

* Hey, where's the rainbow? (Have you ever noticed that when you're facing a rainbow, the sun is always directly behind you?)

* A lot of people say, "When it rains, it pours." What does that mean? (When one bad thing happens, more bad things follow, and usually all at once!) It's also been said "One cloud feels lonely." Is this more accurate?

* There are many areas of the world that are desperate for rain. Crops fail and populations are at risk. We should be thankful for being rained out, right?

PICNICS

I'm sure you don't need instructions on how to have a picnic. But what if it rains the day of the big plan? I suggest simply moving your picnic indoors! Spread a blanket on the floor, maybe near a window. Keep the television off, and use the time to talk to each other. You can watch the rain coming down and take your time having a good meal together.

PARENT-TO-PARENT ASIDE

It's a good idea to talk to your children about carrying through with plans even though something hasn't quite gone as planned. While it might be ok to cancel a picnic once in a while, what if you're having a picnic with a friend who's moving to France tomorrow? In some cases, canceling causes problems. And so it's important to have a Plan B. By planning alternatives, your children will learn to be flexible and to use their imagination.

WHEN YOU'RE HAVING AN INDOOR PICNIC:

* Talk about how it's always good to have alternate plans.
* Ask your children where they'd like to go for an ideal outdoor picnic.
* Ask your children about the advantages of an indoor picnic. (No ants, for example.)
* Talk about the advantages of eating balanced meals. (Better health.)

PLAYGROUND

Many parks, especially local/city parks, have playgrounds. These areas are especially designed to entertain children, so why not take advantage of it? Most parks will have the minimum of swings and a slide. It might not sound like a big adventure to sophisticated adults, but to kids it's hours of fun. There's usually a sandbox too, and younger kids will enjoy making castles and just getting their hands dirty. When you first take your children to the playground, it's a good idea to go over some basic safety rules. For example, only one kid on the steps up the slide at a time, and don't walk in front of or behind the swings. (I've seen more than a few kids get struck when walking unaware in front of a swing.) Of course, you'll get more comfortable with turning them loose as you get accustomed to the playground area, but it never hurts to go over the safety rules occasionally.

PARENT-TO-PARENT ASIDE

When you go to a park you haven't frequented, it's a good idea to walk around and check it out for safety concerns. Make sure there are no sharp edges on the slide and it's well-built. Most swing sets squeak a bit, so that's not a worry, but I have seen seats that look a bit more threadbare than I'm comfortable with. Most swings are situated on tracts of sand or mulch, so most mishaps, such as slipping out of the swing at unexpected times, result mostly in soft landings. But there are other concerns as well. Make sure the area looks generally clean, and there aren't soda pop tops lying around in the sand. Other metallic, glass, or plastic debris can put a quick end to a day of fun at your local park's playground.

WHILE YOU'RE AT THE PLAYGROUND:

* See if your kids would want to bring any of their friends the next time you come to the playground.

* Does your playground have a jungle gym? If so, see who can hang the longest without dropping.

* Ask your kids what they would do if they were designing their own playground.

* What's their favorite activity at the playground?

CHAPTER 4

Overnight Activities

● ●

If you're a divorced parent, then having your children overnight offers more opportunities to enrich your relationship with them. Any amount of time you spend with your kids is precious, but the overnighters allow you to do much more, such as the time-honored traditions of reading bedtime stories, tucking them into bed, and the all important, late-night snacks!

Right after I was divorced, I made a point of keeping my children at least one night a week, usually Friday night. For younger children, this makes it easy for them to remember their next visit to Dad's house. Fridays at Dad's! They'll never have to think twice about whether or not it's an off week with Dad. And when they talk to their friends, it sounds so nice: Fridays at Dad's.

For me, Fridays at Dad's meant many things, all of them enjoyable, memorable, from going outside to watch meteor showers and search for constellations, to camping out in the living room and having leftover pizza for breakfast.

> ## OVERNIGHT ACTIVITIES
> Movie Night
> Reading
> Bath Time
> Build Weekend Storage Boxes
> Weekend Journals

MOVIE NIGHT

When my oldest was eight (over ten years ago!), my children and I started a tradition. Every Friday night I had to come up with an activity to do with my kids, and it became movie night. We would go to the local video rental store, pick out two or three movies depending on their length (make sure to check the playing time of each movie), nuke some popcorn, and rearrange the chairs in the living room in a semi-circle in front of the TV.

Especially if you're a rookie weekend parent, when your children are young, routine is important. They want to know what to expect. Giving them movie night is a wonderful way to add some order to their lives. If your children are still very young, try renting old Disney movies or whatever else you feel is suitable.

PARENT-TO-PARENT ASIDE

I prefer science fiction, action/adventure, and horror movies, and these tend to have violence. While many people argue against exposing children to any violence, I instead simply encourage caution. Your children are exposed to violence and cruelty on a daily basis—for example, in their school playgrounds where they may be teased and taunted and put down. Even in a cartoon movie a horrible event—such as Bambi's mother being shot—can happen. As your children get older, they're going to be exposed to the bad things in this world, even on the six o'clock news. Use your best judgment and talk to your children about your concerns. For them to grow into successful adults, they will need to be able to psychologically deal with the real world. How will your children deal emotionally with the bad stuff unless you give them a context to help them make good decisions?

WHEN YOU HAVE MOVIE NIGHT:

* Take control of the remote. If there's a point in the movie you want to talk about—hit pause. Make your pitch, then go back to play. Your children might get a bit aggravated if you do this

a lot. That's okay. Explain that you feel a need to do some parenting and ask them to please accommodate you.

* Have a post-movie discussion. Who was the bad guy? The good guy? What did the hero want? What obstacles were in his/her way?

* Did the movie remind any of your children of situations in their lives? In what way? Did they get any ideas of how to handle stresses and challenges in their lives? Ask them for examples.

* Take requests for what to rent the next weekend. If they're older, ask them to research their requests and give you a basic overview, including the rating.

READING

Reading books aloud is a great way to spend both entertaining and inexpensive time with your children. This may lose its appeal as your children grow older—but it's always a great idea to spend an extra half an hour reading to your children at bedtime. When they are young, you can start with a Dr. Seuss book—which can be read in barely any time at all. As your children grow up, your collection of books should grow up as well. You don't need to finish a book in a sitting. Even a twelve-year-old will enjoy a chapter of *Maniac Magee* (which is about a 7th grader) or another Newbery Medal winner. With older children, you can take turns reading, and they'll develop their oratory skills while doing it.

Try treasure hunting for books at a flea market or yard sale—perhaps even with your kids. You could also ask at work or within your circle of friends to see if anyone has children that have out-grown their books and would like to donate them to the cause.

PARENT-TO-PARENT ASIDE

At first when I was ferrying three children to my apartment on the weekends, there were so many items we forgot to bring over that it quickly became a source of frustration. I was in luck because my ex-wife only lived a 3-minute drive away. Still, having to make two or three trips was ridiculous. I came up with a plan that involved large containers. My children would just throw all of their stuff into these laundry baskets and we'd hit the road. This also helped with the reverse migration, because they would also have the habit of leaving things at my place and I'd have to do the reverse commute as well. Of course, I gradually acquired dressers for my children and they were able to keep some clothes over at my place.

WHILE YOU'RE READING AT BEDTIME:

* Ask questions about what you've just read.
* Take requests: Is there anything your kids would like to read?
* Why are stories more interesting than cooking recipes?
* If your child is beginning to learn how to read, have him or her read every other page, and read the book together.

THE PRACTICAL GUIDE TO WEEKEND PARENTING

BATH TIME

Your children may outgrow this quickly, but I found this to be an activity that added a definite sense of continuity from day to day for my children. If your child is so young that he/she not only needs help washing but also needs an adult present because of the drowning hazard, it's your responsibility, as you know, to give them a bath. But even as they outgrow this, make them take a bath or shower. I stopped this imperative at some indistinct age that I can't remember (isn't that the way it always is?), but it was a very important weekend regimen at my household for many years. We had a well stocked toy bin with bathroom toys. Plastic ducks. Wind-up boats. Submarines. When I stopped giving baths, my children had already made this a part of their personal pattern.

> **FUN FACT:**
> *Legend has it that Archimedes discovered his famous theory of buoyancy— Archimedes Principle— while taking a bath.*

PARENT-TO-PARENT ASIDE

When my children were very young (and they were all very close in age, too), they were given baths all at once. Eventually, my daughter had to be bathed separately once she began to notice just how different she was from her two brothers. Later still, as the boys need for independence grew, I began giving them separate baths. Children grow. They need space and a sense of identity. You will have to grow with them, be flexible, and adapt to their needs.

WHEN IT'S BATH TIME:

* Talk about why cleanliness and sanitation are important for health reasons. (Germs and bacteria cause sickness and disease.)

* Talk about what went well that day, and also what could've gone better.

* Ask if they'd like to try some bubble bath. (Put it on your shopping list if they do.)

* Why are hot baths considered relaxing, especially to hard-working adults? (They soothe tense muscles and ease tension.)

* Ask if, next time, they'd like to take a shower instead.

BUILD WEEKEND STORAGE BOXES

As an alternative to the laundry baskets you are hauling from house to house, you can try building a box unique to each child to transport their clothes and other essentials. You don't need to make this large, however. This could be a small memento box or something larger for more permanent storage of large items (such as clothes).

You can make this out of several different types of material. If you're in a hurry, just get a cardboard box and decorate it. Or perhaps you could weave ribbons around a laundry basket. Personalize the storage box by drawing patterns on it with permanent markers. Writing their names on the storage boxes will help give them a sense of ownership, which you want to encourage, making your children feel like they have their own personal space in your house.

If you have tools and the inclination, try making it out of wood. You could turn this into a "big kid" project by making a large storage box and using power tools. Of course, power tools are dangerous and you should always observe safety precautions and discuss safety with your children. If you're not handy with tools, perhaps you can ask your friends and try to enlist the aid of someone who can come by and help on this special project. Scout leaders, neighbors, and teachers are also good resources. I've also found that hardware store employees can be extremely helpful.

PARENT-TO-PARENT ASIDE

When your children are still young, an item that will definitely stay in their storage box is their "blankey." You know what it is—the emotional and personal item that Linus carries around. Of my three children, one had a blankey, one had a stuffed animal, and one didn't need anything (nor did he want one). Acknowledge the importance of the favorite item and keep special track of it.

WHILE YOU'RE CONSTRUCTING STORAGE BOXES:

* What would your children put in the box if that box was the only thing they could bring to a deserted island?

* Can your children think of any animal that stores things? What about squirrels? Ants? Spiders? Kangaroos?

* What's a time capsule? Why do people make them? (Time capsules are containers that protect their contents from deteriorating with the effects of time for centuries. They're used for many reasons, from leaving mementos to future descendents to making an investment in future historical understanding.)

* Talk about making your own time capsule, which will be put away for a period of time (discuss what time they feel would be reasonable) to open later. What would your children put in it?

WEEKEND JOURNALS

Encourage your kids to write in a weekend journal. If they seem uncomfortable with this, try making a rule that they only have to write in it once per weekend, and their entry can be as short as one sentence—and that you won't peek at what they write. This writing is for their benefit, not yours. When I suggested this journal idea to my youngest son, he seemed unsure about it. When I promised not to peek, and said that he was able to write whatever he wanted, he became much more enthusiastic about the concept. Perhaps he wrote about our conversation in the journal. I wouldn't know.

I'm a stickler for routines. Good habits, too. Try to develop a good routine in the evenings such as writing in a journal, brushing teeth, going to bed, then reading.

PARENT-TO-PARENT ASIDE

Children need to learn to write "more better." Do you know what I mean? The more your child writes, the better the writing. Practice makes perfect. There are many ways to encourage writing. Reading a lot helps a child understand the ways in which words are put together and can improve a child's comfort level with writing. Make a special trip to the store for a special ink pen that's only for journal use. Try out several different kinds of pens. Computers have, of course, made keyboards a writing instrument, and I've discovered that instant messaging has been a boon to my youngest child's interest in writing. Have them write down phone messages, directions to an after-school event, shopping lists, and thank-you letters for birthday presents.

WHILE YOU'RE DISCUSSING JOURNALS:

* Why is it that sometimes people don't know how they're feeling about a subject until they begin talking or writing about it? (Writing helps us sort out our thoughts.)

* Are some things important to remember? How can everything that's important be remembered (by someone who doesn't nec-

essarily have a photographic memory)? (I know I can't remember *everything* that's important, which is why I write it down.)

* Why do people find the journals of Anne Frank interesting? (Anne Frank was hunted by the Nazis. People want to read about her feelings during that perilous period of time.)

* Tell your children that it's sometimes fun to draw small pictures in their journals.

* Ask: "If you had to describe today with one word, what would it be?"

CHAPTER 5

Road Trip

• •

There's a wonderful opportunity for activities in the car when you're driving somewhere. The activities in this chapter are for while you're on the road. Of course, driving safely is always the number one consideration.

Driving is a fact of life for most of us. We've become so busy in the hustle and bustle of daily life that we don't have time to walk or go by bicycle. Our primary mode of transportation is the automobile. But now you can turn this fact of life into your parenting advantage.

You have a captive audience! There's no television (although more and more vehicles each year come equipped with DVD players) to distract them. Use this time for activities that let you bond with your kids. Not only that, it'll be fun!

ROAD TRIP ACTIVITIES

Car Games

Round Robin Stories

U.S. Patent Awards

Tongue Twisters

Discuss a Topic

CAR GAMES

When you're bored in the car during a long trip, there are more exciting things to do other than sing "The Wheels on the Bus Go Round and Round" for hours. While there are some games that have been around for ages (such as "I Spy" or "20 Questions,") you should also be inventive and try new things. My children have come up with games that I never played as a child. There's one game where they hit each other on the shoulder whenever they spot a Volkswagen Beetle, called Slug Bug.

Some other games:

* Count license plates from different states.

* Find the vehicle with the most tires.

* Everyone pick a color and count "their" vehicles.

* Search for different kinds of trucks and announce what they're used for.

* Count road signs, mile markers, and the first to a hundred wins!

PARENT-TO-PARENT ASIDE

We've all seen the competitive nature in people. Some of it is good, some bad. But no matter what, learning to compete is an important part of the maturation process. As adults, for example, we compete for jobs with other job applicants. This is why playing games is important for children. It's important to note, though, that sometimes people go too far. Not everything is a competition. While you're on the road, point out to your children how some motorists drive unsafely because of competing to get ahead of other drivers.

WHILE YOU'RE PLAYING A CAR GAME:

* Ask your children if they understand why safety is so important while riding in a car.

* Tell your children to ask their friends and see if they can come up with some new games to play while riding in a car.

* If you've had a stressful day, make a game out of who can go the longest without talking or giggling. After a few minutes, giggle.

* Tell them you need some information, and have them read parts of the owner's manual to you.

* Have them count how many buttons and knobs are inside the car.

ROUND ROBIN STORIES

This is a fun and entertaining way to keep the entire car occupied for long—or even short—periods. It's simple to start and involves everyone. Have someone (perhaps an adult) begin creating a story, and get about three or four sentences into it before "tagging" the person to their right. It's then their turn to continue it. Watch how interesting it is to see what will change from person to person, often in interesting and curious ways.

PARENT-TO-PARENT ASIDE

This round-robin storytelling activity can of course be done in places other than your car. I've found that this can help draw out shy children. While quieter children often get drowned out by the more boisterous ones, this activity gives everybody an equal opportunity to have his or her voice heard. As a sort of aside to this aside, I've done this activity when not only my children are in the car, but one or two of their friends. This helps their friends relate to me and it helps me understand the nature of my children's friends. Everybody wins with this activity.

WHILE YOU'RE STORYTELLING:

* At the end of the story, discuss how the story changed from storyteller to storyteller.

* Explain how the tall tales of Paul Bunyan and Pecos Bill are different from how a story changes in round-robin storytelling. (Folklore characters like Paul Bunyan and Pecos Bill arise from exaggerated storytelling, which was a popular form of entertainment before the days of television.)

* Change the style of storytelling. For one round, everyone have humorous sections. The next round, sad. Try exciting, edge-of-your seat storytelling.

* See if anybody can include words that rhyme during storytelling.

* Try a round-robin poem. Everybody says two lines of a poem. The first line rhymes with the last line from the previous storyteller.

U.S. PATENT AWARDS

When you're on the road, take a look at your surroundings for inspiration. Talk to your children about the inventions they see in daily life that they might not even recognize. For example, who came up with the idea of turn signal lights on sideview mirrors? Why did this get incorporated into newer car designs?

Try to get your children to begin thinking about their own process or design that might be patentable. Discuss what would be patentable. What makes an idea a good idea? Is it that it'll make money? Or that it will improve people's lives by making something safer or easier to do?

PARENT-TO-PARENT ASIDE

Some children may be more scientifically inclined than others. That's all right. The important thing is to present your children with different opportunities to explore their interests, and being so young, they may not know exactly what their interests are. It's tempting to try to steer children in the direction of a parent's interests, but this road often leads to frustration. It's so much better to have children discover their own interests and talents. Parents should try to offer different options and encourage exploration of various pursuits.

WHILE YOU'RE DOING THE "PATENT CHALLENGE":

* Talk about the patents that have had the greatest effect on our lives. What would it be? The light bulb? The telegraph?

* If your children could invent anything (and were guaranteed it would work), what would they invent? (Try to let your children answer before prompting them with ideas. They might surprise you!)

* If a design could either make people more comfortable or it could make lots of money, which would your children choose?

* Ask your children what "patent pending" means. (A patent has been applied for but not yet granted.)

* Ask them to find a product that has a label with a U.S. patent number on it and point it out to you.

TONGUE TWISTERS

A good way to get gaggles of giggles while driving is by reciting tongue twisters out loud. Try to say them fast, again and again. This can be fun in the car—but don't get distracted from your driving safely!

Here are some I remember most:

Peter Piper picked a peck of pickled peppers. If Peter Piper picked a peck of pickled peppers, where's the peck of pickled peppers Peter Piper picked?

Sally sells shiny seashells by the seashore.

How much wood could a woodchuck chuck if a woodchuck could chuck wood?

Rubber baby buggy bumpers.

Freshly fried fat flying fish.

Betty bought butter but the butter was bitter, so Betty bought better butter to make the bitter butter better.

Six sick snakes sit by the sea.

PARENT-TO-PARENT ASIDE

Once you get your children talking with these tongue twisters, ask them questions, lots of questions. Many times, when asked about their day, your kids will shrug and give non-answers. It's good to do a little digging. Think about it this way: Their lives are buried treasures and you can only uncover them by scraping and digging away layer after layer of soil. It's not necessarily true that they are purposefully covering anything up. Many times, they simply don't know what kind of information you're looking for. Remember, they don't know what is important to you. Here are some examples: Who's their favorite teacher? Why? Who's their best friend at school? Did anyone get in trouble at school today? Are their teachers fair? Do they discuss politics? Are there any bullies at school?

While You're Twisting Your Tongue:

* Make sure to laugh at the mistakes—especially your own.

* See if your children can make up their own tongue twisters.

* What makes a tongue twister different than a sentence that all begins with the same letter? (Tongue twisters begin with the same sound—phoneme in phonics—while a sentence that begins with the same letter doesn't necessarily all sound alike.)

* What makes a good tongue twister? (One that really twists your tongue in knots!)

DISCUSS A TOPIC

Try having a discussion topic of the week. It might be a good idea to let your children know the topic in advance so they can try to get some information. This discussion can be about anything, and I often conduct these in the car while traveling here and there doing "taxi-service" obligations.

One of your responsibilities as a weekend parent is to get your children to think for themselves. Having a discussion (especially one in which there's a question posed and there's no "right" answer) is a good way to do this while still having quality time together. Try discussing why there isn't a higher graduation rate, or what is the best way to balance the national budget. What's the best sport, and why? Who would win in a battle between Godzilla and the Martians from *War of the Worlds*?

PARENT-TO-PARENT ASIDE

Getting your children to think for themselves is important. I knew a parent who thought good grades were paramount. He ended up "doing" the homework and projects for his children so they'd get good grades. Yes, his kids went off to college, but they dropped out their freshman years and moved back into—yes, you guessed it—the parent's house. (Some parents may secretly want this—there is such a thing as empty nest syndrome.) Don't fall prey to this trap—for your kids' sakes.

WHILE YOU'RE DISCUSSING:

* Do their teachers ever have important discussions about non-academic subjects?

* Is there anything that should be discussed later, when there's more information available? (Sometimes it's better to wait for the facts instead of speculating.)

* Why are discussions so important? (It's how we learn how and what others think!)

* What does the term "a meeting of the minds" mean? Are discussions important in achieving this? (A meeting of the minds means that there's a mutual understanding. Discussions help achieve this.)

CHAPTER 6

Local Fun

Want to get out of the house? There are often many fun-filled activities only a short drive away. You might be surprised by the variety of nearby activities you can find to do with your children. Some will cost a little money, but you don't have to go overboard. Maybe do an activity that costs money every other weekend, or perhaps once a month. By exposing your children to the activities in this chapter, you'll be giving them experiences that they'll remember the rest of their lives, and everyone will have fun!

Although this book is handy for the moments when you're searching for something to do with your children, the activities in this chapter also can help give your children an exciting reason to look forward to the weekend if you plan these activities in advance. For example, if you tell your children that you're planning a trip to the bowling alley for next weekend, they'll be talking about it all week with their friends. They'll greet the weekend with big smiles. So when you can, give your kids a treat. Of course, it's not a bad idea to ask your children which activity they prefer, but I suggest trying all of them, and if there's one activity they frown at, tell them to humor you and go along and then the next weekend they can pick the activity.

LOCAL FUN ACTIVITIES

Miniature Golf • Bowling • Hiking • Sports • Libraries
Swimming • Shopping • Showtime • Movie Theater
Flea Markets • Yard Sales • Roller Skating

MINIATURE GOLF

If it's a beautiful day outside, consider taking your children—and their friends—to the miniature golf course. This can teach your children hand/eye coordination, teamwork, and even gives you a chance to get some old-fashioned exercise outdoors.

Before heading out on the road, talk to your children to decide which golf course to play at. If there's a conflict, negotiate a compromise. If that doesn't seem possible, try writing the ideas on a piece of paper and drawing one blindly from a hat. Remind your kids that the next time golf is scheduled, the other idea will be used.

If you have a large number of children playing, it's a good idea to make teams so that there are multiple "winners." When splitting into teams, try placing yourself on the same team as the youngest putter. Try this or other combinations to make the competition even. It's usually not a great idea to let your children select their own teams, so it's a wise parent that looks ahead and finds easy, non-offensive ways to choose teammates. As an example, try playing "shoes versus sandals."

In miniature golf, the low score wins. If you're planning to return, keep individual scores so that the next time you play, there can be a "handicap." For example, if the weekend parent wins by ten strokes over Child #1 and five strokes over Child #2, then at the start of the next game, the parent begins with a stroke count of ten and Child #2 begins with a stroke count of five. This handicap is designed in such a way that the second game should end in a tie (unless someone improves or is lucky!).

PARENT-TO-PARENT ASIDE

When you're playing miniature golf, take the opportunity to teach your children the lesson about ties. We live in a world where there always seems to be a winner and a loser. It's the competitive nature of capitalism. Try sitting down and discussing that being the "best" doesn't always mean having a winning score. Sometimes everyone wins. Wouldn't it be wonderful if we lived in a world in which everyone realized that by teamwork and working together, we could all be winners?

While You're Putting:

* Ask your children if they know what "par" means. (It is the average number of strokes it takes to complete a hole.)

* Discuss how much practice Tiger Woods had to do as a youngster in order to become one of the world's premier golfers. How old was Tiger when he started? (2 years old.)

* If "par" is the average, why do so many professional golfers have scores that are over par? (Par requires errorless play, and because there are 18 holes in a golf course, there are 18 opportunities to make mistakes.)

* A "birdie" is one stroke under par on any particular hole. When one of your kids scores a birdie, say "tweet tweet."

* Think about the strategy of the game. For example, the person who scores the lowest on the previous hole putts first on the next. What's the disadvantage? (The players putting next can "play it safe" if the first putter messes up by landing in or hitting an obstacle.)

BOWLING

There are a lot of concerns with bowling that mimic those you read about in "Miniature Golf." For example, you should be concerned with making teams fair and using handicaps to even the scores. Try pulling up the bumpers for even more fun! Make this a true family outing, invite your kid's friends, and make an afternoon of it. Depending on where you live, this may need a short car trip.

If bowling is a new activity for you and the kids, the scoring system may be confusing. Most bowling alleys will calculate it for you on electronic screens, but they won't be able to give you more obscure rules. Interest your children in learning more and provide them with sources to find that information. If you have Internet access, you can find scoring rules there. Otherwise, take them to the library. You can even make it a challenge: Tell your children your plans to bowl in advance and have them find out and instruct you on the rules.

PARENT-TO-PARENT ASIDE

When you empower your children to go on fact-finding missions, such as Learn How to Score a Game of Bowling, you win. I'm still learning so many things (thank goodness for the History Channel!) that it's theoretically impossible to teach my children everything I know. They'll never catch up! One of your most important tasks is to teach your children how to learn—and more importantly, to love it. At some point, they will be on their own, and it often occurs earlier than you initially envisioned.

WHILE YOU'RE BOWLING:

* See if there's a list of high scorers at the bowling alley.
* Is there an advantage to using a heavy bowling ball or a light one?
* Compare scores. Discuss how many pins need to get knocked down to catch up to the first-place bowler. (A great fun way to practice math.)

HIKING

While a traditional hike takes place on a nature trail, don't feel hemmed in by that. It's just as fun to take a hike through a city. I've found that having a "destination" helps the children focus on that goal. My kids have argued with me in the past that just "walking" seems pointless. That's fine—set the goal to be to hike to the Goodwill store ten blocks away. Or to the Dairy Queen down the block. Or a particular store. Or hike to a park (where you can then rest under a tree).

If you do find a park, have your children search and point out to you at least three interesting things in nature. These can be as simple as a spider's web, a bird's nest, or unusual vegetation. Make it an adventure! Regardless if you end up in a park or not, you should take time to talk about what you see, from cars to buildings to unusual leaves on the trees.

FUN FACT: *Hiking the Appalachian Trail might take you quite a while; it is 2,160 miles long.*

PARENT-TO-PARENT ASIDE

Healthy lifestyles are becoming more important in a world in which we find ourselves increasingly sitting down, inactive in front of computers, video games, and a television. Walking is great exercise! So taking a hike isn't just fun, it helps us develop healthy habits by being active.

WHILE YOU'RE HIKING:

* Talk about what it must've been like before the age of the automobile. How would it have affected the world? How about the mail system? (There's no right answer here. Just have fun and discuss.)

* How important is the proper footwear when you are walking? (Not only does proper footwear protect your feet from broken glass and rusty nails, it helps absorb the shock of foot striking ground.)

* How would you measure your average speed? Take a guess, then time your walk and estimate the distance you travel (or better yet, buy a pedometer).

* What would you expect to see different if your hike was during a different season of the year? (Describe what makes the seasons different from each other.)

SPORTS

There are high school and middle school sporting events that take place year round. Many communities—maybe even your own—have minor league baseball teams. Some sports will even skip the entrance fee. There are also community leagues. One of the most memorable games I ever watched was between two baseball teams in a city league. I have no idea who won, but the stakes appeared high because all of the players were intensely into the game. Their level of athleticism, while hovering only slightly above "competent," was nonetheless spirited and interesting. Check your local newspapers for listings, or call up your local school system for details.

PARENT-TO-PARENT ASIDE

Good sportsmanship is an essential point to teach when you are raising a child. While no one particularly enjoys losing a sporting event, it's important to teach the art of losing. Nobody wins at everything during their lifetime. Learning to accept loss is essential. Feel free to feel remorse at not winning, but learn to accept it and move on. There's always "next season" or "we'll get 'em next time." And since nothing can be done about a call made by an official or referee, it makes no sense to get upset over it. Please remember that while many parents preach good sportsmanship to their children, some will sit in the stands and scream and yell at the officials and coaches. This is a "show by example" thing. Your children learn by mimicking you as much as by listening to your words.

WHILE YOU'RE AT A SPORTING EVENT:

* Talk about the rules of the game. Why are there arguments on a particular call from an official/referee? (People see the play from different angles, so sometimes a foul from one angle looks like a non-foul from another.)

* Which team has the best uniforms? Why?

* Does one team show more teamwork? Does one team appear more talented?

* What are the coaches doing? How involved are they in the game?

* Are the teams showing good sportsmanship? What is good sportsmanship?

* Ask who your children's favorite athletes are.

* Can you come up with your own cheer?

* Why are people sad when they lose a sporting event? Why do teams shake hands after a sporting event? (To show good sportsmanship and respect.)

LIBRARIES

Check with your library and see if your children can get library cards. A library is a great place to browse. Many libraries also have fun reading programs for young children, and sometimes for teens, too. If your children aren't enthused about picking out a book, send them to the periodical section where magazines are free for perusing. Encourage your children to find what they enjoy reading, and don't force them to read books. Looking for the latest update on a professional sports team? Try *Sports Illustrated*. Wanting to fix up the house or yard? *Home Living* will suit your needs. If your child enjoys video games, magazines such as *Electronic Gaming* and *Game Informer* provide great reading material.

The goal here is to get your children reading. It will help their grades and increase their self-esteem. A whole new world opens for your kids when they begin reading. They can discover that there are other people who feel and think the way that they do.

If you know of a particularly good bookstore in your area, whether it sells new or used books, think about giving your children a "book allowance."

PARENT-TO-PARENT ASIDE

Most parents have fixed budgets and are lacking what I call an excess of monetary funds. It's crucial to spend money on the necessities, but I've always been of the belief that providing a reading library for my kids was incredibly important. Take some of the money that goes into your rainy day fund and spend it on books.

WHILE YOU'RE AT THE LIBRARY:

* Talk (whispering, of course) about what kind of books interests your children. Fiction? Nonfiction? Books about crafts? Teenage books? Harry Potter?

* Talk about the responsibility of owning a library card. Who will pay for late fees (and how)?

* Where does the money come from to build a library and stock it with books? (Mostly from local and regional sources, but the state governments chip in, too, as well as some federal government grants.)

* Learn the various sections of a library. What's the Dewey Decimal System? Does your library still have a card catalog? Or do you find books via a computer terminal? (The Dewey Decimal System is a way for organizing library books into 10 numerical categories, such as 300–399 for books about social sciences.)

* Encourage your kids to talk to the librarian if there are any questions about the library. Librarians are typically very helpful (and they know a lot about books!).

SWIMMING

Swimming is a great skill to have—and potentially life-saving. If there are lessons given by a local YMCA or other organization, you should take advantage of them. Drowning is the second leading cause of injury-related death of children under the age of fifteen. It's not enough to teach your children how to swim; take the extra time to teach water safety. There are many sources of information on water safety, and learning water safety itself can be a family project (with perhaps a prize of a beach trip as motivation).

PARENT-TO-PARENT ASIDE

I should note that drowning occurs in younger children in bathtubs and shallow pools (and even toilets), where swimming isn't the issue. Parent awareness and supervision around water is of the utmost importance. Remember that small children (even older ones) can panic, so it's a good idea to keep an eye on them even if the situation looks safe enough. And as your children get older and begin learning how to swim, be sure to watch them yourself so you can make a judgment about their abilities. Challenge them to become a better swimmer than you.

WHILE YOU'RE AT THE POOL OR BEACH:

* Play "Marco Polo." (Conduct research to learn this popular game!)

* At the beach, discuss the nature and structure of sand castles. Build one as a team project. Have everyone build his/her own. Why did people need to build castles in Europe? (To hold power in conquered territory, intimidate local populations, offer places of refuge, and provide safe places for rulers to live.)

* What's the purpose of a moat? (To make approaching the castle wall difficult and to prevent someone digging under the wall.)

* What's a danger of overexposure to UV rays from the sun? How can you protect against this? (Sunburns can cause serious injury. Protect with clothes and sunscreen lotion.)

* Bring a picnic lunch. Talk about health concerns of storing food in warm weather.

* Why do they put chlorine in public pools? (To disinfect and sanitize the water, and to stop algae growth.)

* Why are the oceans salty? Why are the lakes not salty? Why is the Great Salt Lake in Utah an exception? (Lakes are filled with rainwater, from which the salt has been removed by evaporation. The Great Salt Lake gets its salt from rivers carrying salts leached from the soil and rocks unique to the area.)

* How dangerous is water pollution? What can be done at home to keep our waters clean? (Pollution can destroy water habitats and make water undrinkable. Properly disposing of household chemicals and batteries can help prevent dangerous chemicals leaching into groundwater from landfills. Don't be a litterbug!)

SHOPPING

This may seem to be a silly suggestion, but malls can be fascinating places to visit—and most of them have a bookstore! You can find specialty shops with pieces of handcrafted art, or bargain (dollar) stores. A mall can be a good place to go because children instinctively like to be there. You will have a lot of free time while walking from store to store, during which you can "talk" to your kids. If you are worried about your children wanting to purchase toys or any other things, I suggest going window shopping and not actually enter the stores. Another option is to give them a spending allowance before you go.

PARENT-TO-PARENT ASIDE

There's a stage that children go through during which "I want" seems to be the first two words of every spoken sentence. This can be rough during trips to stores. Let's face it: Commercials are designed to make children want those items that look like so much fun on television. Because my trips to the store with my children were seldom more than once a week, I usually allowed one item per child, given that it didn't hurt my budget. If it is an expensive item, explain how the child can save money over a period of time and buy the item later, or suggest searching for the item at a yard sale or flea market.

If you're honest with your children about why they can't have something in particular, they might throw a tantrum, but they'll sense that you're being fair with them, and it's not a bad idea to explain to them how you're being fair. Of course, if a child acts up in public, going to the car or home immediately is a good option. They'll learn that the behavior is unacceptable and that you won't stand for it.

WHILE YOU'RE AT THE MALL:

* Find something that you want to buy if someday you get rich.

* Ask your children to name their three most favorite stores.

* Is there anything they can find in the mall that they are willing to work around the house for in order to earn money to buy?

SHOTIME

There are many school plays performed during the school year, as well as community and civic centers hosting events of all kinds. A lot of cities have "concerts in the park." Make it a "Big To Do." Find them in the newspaper. Call your chamber of commerce for help in locating these events. Many are free or inexpensive.

PARENT-TO-PARENT ASIDE

My musical ability is near zero. I have no ear for it. However, I've always encouraged my children to learn to play a musical instrument when the opportunity arises in their schools. It helps them learn teamwork (everyone playing together to perform a piece of music). It helps them with math—remember, musical notes are written on a scale with lots of terms like eighth notes and a three-four beat. And whenever they play, I nod my head and say it sounds great (who am I to say otherwise?). If nothing else, buy a harmonica and have your children learn to play a simple song on it. All 3 of my children have developed considerable musical abilities, perhaps because they simply had a chance to try different instruments.

WHILE YOU'RE AT THE PLAY/SHOW/CONCERT, EITHER WAITING FOR IT TO BEGIN OR ON YOUR WAY THERE:

* Talk to your kids about how television studios might broadcast the event.

* Pose a question, like: How much practice did the performers need to put on the show?

* Would any of your children want to try their hand at acting or playing a musical instrument?

> **FUN FACT:**
> In 543 BC, a Greek named Thespis became the first actor, which is why today's actors are referred to as thespians.

MOVIE THEATER

Taking your children to the movies provides a good opportunity to talk about morals, ethics—and maybe even homework. The trip to the theater usually brings up other movies that they've seen, providing a good opportunity also to talk about the moral and ethical decisions that were made by the characters—even cartoon characters—in those movies. For me, the opportunity to talk about homework came as a simple matter of having free time with them (away from the television). There's the time spent in the car going to the theater and the time in your seat before the movie starts.

Theaters have increased their ticket prices (steadily, it seems), so you might want to eat before you go. I suggest sharing a bag of popcorn and a drink for the feature. Tell your children that sharing food symbolically makes you a "family." It's where the expression "breaking bread" comes from. And it never hurts to promote sharing among your children.

Theaters usually have matinee prices, so going before certain times of day will save money on ticket prices. Call ahead to see when matinee prices are in effect.

PARENT-TO-PARENT ASIDE

Depending on the movie, you might want to watch the movie before your children to see if it's appropriate for their age groups. The film's MPAA rating is supposed to help guide you by identifying appropriate age groups. For example, "G" is for general audiences and is usually a safe bet that there won't be any offensive or inappropriate material in the film. Still, you might want to check online for websites that offer suggestions for kid-friendly movies. For example, www.parentpreviews.com is a website that offers parents feedback on several aspects of a movie's kid-friendliness, including violence, sexual content, language, and drugs/alcohol.

WHILE YOU'RE RETURNING HOME FROM THE MOVIE:

* Have your children describe their three favorite parts of the movie. Do the same to kick the conversation off.

* Was there a difficult decision that the hero or heroine had to make? What decision was it? What were the pros and cons of the decision? Would any of your children do it differently?

* Ask your children how they would have made the outcome of the movie different if they had directed it.

* Did the characters in the movie have control of their destiny? What can your children do to get better control of their destinies?

FLEA MARKETS

One up from yard sales, flea markets can make a great place to do some searching for larger pieces of furniture—perhaps you can plan a complete re-decoration of a kid's playroom with what you find. While you might be able to hike to the nearest yard sale, flea markets might be farther away and require the use of a car.

Flea markets provide a great opportunity to teach your children about bargaining skills. While a retail store's prices are set, the items you find in a flea market or yard sale are typically being sold by individuals. Suggest to the seller that the price be dropped by a dollar. If someone is selling four videos for 10 dollars, say you'll accept if it's five videos.

PARENT-TO-PARENT ASIDE

One of the most difficult aspects of life to teach children is the value of money. There are several ways to attack the problem. One is an allowance. Another is to participate with your children on searching for bargains. If, for example, the new school year is approaching and you're in the market for new clothes, discuss a budget you're your children. Go over advertisements in the newspaper. Search bargain stores. Children will see how, for a given amount of money, their purchasing power can be dramatically increased by finding bargains. It'll help them understand the value of a dollar and save you money.

WHILE YOU'RE AT A FLEA MARKET:

* Assign a project for your children to find out where the term "flea market" comes from. (The name comes from an old French marketplace called "Market of the Fleas" in which goods were thought to attract flea-laden rodents. The marketplace was, however, quite popular.)

* Ask your children what the difference between a flea market and a yard sale is. (When people sell their own used items in their own yards, it's a yard sale. At flea markets, there are a

THE PRACTICAL GUIDE TO WEEKEND PARENTING

variety of vendors and many typically offer items for sale that aren't used.)

* Look for crafts for sale. See if you can get ideas for weekend craft projects to do with your children.

YARD SALES

Sometimes you'll see signs advertising a yard sale on the side of the road. These impromptu side trips can be fun, whether you are on the way to the park or to Grandma's house. If you'd like to plan your Saturday afternoon sale-hunt, try looking through the announcements in the local newspapers. Not only can you save money, you can get some great fixer-upper project ideas to do with your children. For example, you can buy a desk that is only two dollars (because it has a broken leg). See if your children can come up with a plan to fix it. If your kids are older, see if they can fix it on their own.

PARENT-TO-PARENT ASIDE

One day I took my kids to yard sales and the subject of bullies came up. While, for the most part, I believe avoiding a bully is the way to go, when there's a bully on the school bus, that bully is difficult to avoid. I asked them what they thought their options were before giving my own advice (which was an adult should be notified and the bully should be avoided in the future). My daughter pointed out, however, that the bully would continue to pick on you as long as you don't stand up for yourself. The correct response to a taunt, according to my daughter, is not to turn the other cheek—it's to come right back with a retort. And maybe she's right. This is a decision you need to make based upon who your child is—can you trust your child not to go "too far"? If a bully is stealing your kid's lunch money and your kid does nothing to fight back—well, he is going to be out of a lot of lunches.

WHILE YOU'RE AT A YARD SALE:

* Is there anything you or your children would really like to find?

* What makes the price of an item a "fair" price? (A price is fair when both seller and buyer are satisfied with it and when you don't consider the seller's profit excessive.)

* What are the reasons that people are selling? Are they moving? Did they outgrow an item? Will your children sell toys they've outgrown?

* Talk about organizing your own yard sale.

ROLLER SKATING

You can easily find old pairs of roller skates at yard sales if you don't want to spend the cash on a new pair and you don't know if your children will enjoy it. Once you do, your children can roller skate right outside your home/apartment—as long as you verify it's safe to do so. If your children are old enough, they might prefer inline skates, made popular by the Rollerblade company. In either case, make sure they wear pads!

If you're looking for just an afternoon, look through the telephone book to find roller skating rinks. Rent a pair of skates and go out on the rink with your children. Be patient at first in helping your children learn to roller-skate. It might take a few visits to the rink, but eventually your children will appreciate learning this new skill. This process is one they'll need to repeat often as they grow into mature adults. You could also try ice skating, although ice skating requires much better balance.

FUN FACT:
A Belgian inventor made the first roller skate in 1760 and it was actually an inline skate design.

PARENT-TO-PARENT ASIDE

Roller skating provides another opportunity to spend time away from television and video games. It also provides an opportunity to talk to your children about the value of exercise and being healthy. Roller skating is great exercise, and exercise helps makes us healthy. It was Aristotle who talked about the pleasure of having a "healthy mind in a healthy body." So you can explain to your children that the healthy nature promoted by the latest exercise fad was recognized as important thousands of years ago.

WHILE YOU'RE ROLLER SKATING:

* If you go to a roller rink and rent skates, try marathon skating. See how long you can stay out on the rink before needing a rest.

* For young children, hold their hands.

* Younger children usually start with roller skates. Ask them if they'd like to "graduate" eventually to inline skates. If they do, make a mental note for your Christmas or Birthday list.

CHAPTER 7

Long Distance Adventures

Why go through all the time and trouble of driving someplace farther away? While I've listed many activities for you around the house and close to home, there are several advantages to having activities that are more distant. The first is simply availability. You might not have a local museum, and so this activity implies travel. But it's a worthwhile effort. But in a larger sense, this extended traveling implies an "adventure" simply by the distance. It's not everyday that you drive so far, and so children know that it's a special occasion—an adventure!

The long distance you'll need to travel for these activities gives you and your children an opportunity to plan for trip as well. And planning the trip with your children will help the bonding process. After all, planning for the adventure can be almost as exciting as the adventure itself. It's an activity that you'll be doing as a family. I suggest planning at a table, somewhere away from the television, maybe in the kitchen.

And of course, being in the car with your children for an extended period of time allows you to talk with them. As I've said before, car trips allow for great chances to have talks with your kids. Check the "Road Trip" chapter (page 55) for tips on conversation topics!

LONG DISTANCE ACTIVITIES
Museums • State Park • Festival, Carnival, or Circus
Gemstone Hunting • Boat Racing

MUSEUMS

Local museums are sometimes free or low cost, and they have activity days specially designed for children. Do some investigating in your area. Not only is this an activity that will help you grow closer to your children, museums can be exceptionally educational. I suggest picking up pamphlets and literature that describes what you saw at the museum, and quizzing your kids and talking about the exhibits on the drive home.

Here's a brief list of museums that may fit.

My List of "Museums" Includes:

* Children's Museum
* Science Museum
* Art Museum
* Aquarium
* History Museum
* War Museum
* Smithsonian
* Zoo

PARENT-TO-PARENT ASIDE

As your children grow older, it's likely they will become more involved with school activities. What that means for you is that they'll need more rides home after school, to events, to practice, and to games. By the time they are teenagers, you might be getting a bit tired of this. I suggest talking with the parents of children attending the same events. Set up a carpool. This can also be a great way to get to know your children's friends, which is especially important when they're entering their teen years.

STATE PARK

State parks are generally free to use, unadvertised, and a great place to explore. You can go for hikes and picnics. Some parks have fishing, canoeing, nature walks, and swimming. I suggest calling ahead to get information on what activities are available. You can also get information from your state's park system website, which can be easily found with an Internet search engine and typing in "state parks" with the name of your state. Or, some websites such as www.campgrounds-by-city.com will offer you a list of state parks.

> **FUN FACT:**
> *Mill Ends Park, a city park in Portland, Oregon, is the world's smallest and is only 2 feet wide!*

PARENT-TO-PARENT ASIDE

Going to a state park gives you a chance to talk with your children about having respect for the environment. Ever see litter while walking on a trail? It's not a good sight. Talk to them about Earth Day. Earth Day is celebrated on the first day of spring (in the southern hemisphere, fall) and was established as a global holiday to remind us that conserving natural resources is important for the preservation of Earth. While talking to your children about how recycling is important, the point is better made when you have the fine example of how beautiful nature can be when unspoiled.

WHILE YOU'RE AT THE STATE PARK:

* Stop in the visitor's center. Often these are filled with fun information such as brochures about animal habitats, local plant life, etc.

* If there's a trail map, go on a hike.

* Find a park ranger. Ask if the ranger knows any interesting stories about the park that aren't in the promotional brochures.

* Bring along a book that can help you identify plants, birds, or trees. See how many different kinds you can find.

FESTIVAL, CARNIVAL, OR CIRCUS

There are many places to find a street festival, carnival, or circus. You can try a local college or university for a fall festival, or visit neighboring county fairs. There are some festivals that celebrate various cultures around the world. I suggest looking through local newspapers as a prime source.

Carnivals and circuses can introduce young children to animals they might not have seen before. Definitely bring a camera and take lots of pictures—later you will be able to relive your experiences or spend more time with your children by creating a scrapbook or collage.

PARENT-TO-PARENT ASIDE

Organizations such as 4-H can help get your children involved in local fairs. Another way is to volunteer for a church booth. When you take your kids to these events, talk to them about getting involved and see if there's an information booth that interests them enough into volunteering for next year's event.

WHILE YOU'RE AT THE FESTIVAL/CARNIVAL/CIRCUS:

* Go on a ride with your children.
* See if there are any painting crafts that can be done there.
* Find a memento to bring home to place in your kid's scrapbook. It doesn't have to be purchased. This could be a ticket stub or newspaper advertisement.

GEMSTONE HUNTING

This is a project that can be done in your very backyard. You can order inexpensive gemstones by mail, and then hide them throughout the yard, or (for younger children) in a sandbox. Gemstones and rocks don't need to be valuable, money-wise, in order to be treasures for younger children. Give them praise if they find a particularly colorful rock, or one with an unusual shape. Or, as another option in some states, you can find actual gemstone mines by searching the Internet for them. If you decide to actually visit a gemstone mine, bring a treasure sack (it could be a plastic Ziploc bag or an empty coffee can with a cloth handle stapled onto it) to collect your rocks or gemstones. Plan this as an all-day trip, regardless of age group. Whether you get them from mail order or from an actual mine, be sure to put your rocks and gemstones in a glass or mason jar for display.

PARENT-TO-PARENT ASIDE

Parenting is an expensive venture. From diapers to school clothes, the costs never seem to go away. And with the increasing popularity of cell phones, music recording devices such as MP3 players, and portable game systems, the pressure to buy things for our children has never been greater. It seems we get so caught up with buying the "necessities" that we have no money left when it comes to optional purchases like gemstones for gemstone hunting, especially when it's not something your children specifically asked for. But compared to, say, the price of a computer game, buying a collection of gemstones is a good deal. It will provide you and your children with an activity that everybody will remember as a very special day.

WHILE YOU'RE ROCK/GEMSTONE HUNTING:

* Talk about why some rocks/gemstones are valuable and some aren't.
* Talk about birthstones. What are theirs?

* Why do crystals play such a role in alternative health methods? (Gemstones are believed to be guides for different electromagnetic energies that assist the healing process.)

* Why does light scatter through polished crystals into rainbow colors? (When light travels from one medium to another, such as air into crystal, it bends, and the different colors bend at different angles, creating rainbow colors.)

* Why do rainbows form when it rains? (The raindrops takes sunlight passing through them and breaks it up into seven colors, much like a prism does.)

* Talk about the Gold Rush in the Western United States in the 1800s.

BOAT RACING

For many people, finding water access can be a long-distance adventure. It's a worthwhile endeavor to search for a place where you can test out your home-built boat. Find a park or public access with a pond or lake. You can design sailboats and race to the other side. And if you happen to live near a river, stream, or ditch, you can build boats with the idea of having them race downriver, the current carrying them along. And if you don't live near water, you can always fill up the bathtub (or get a small wading pool), build sailboats and blow air out of your mouths or through a straw to sail them across. Make sure to give prizes for several categories (best design, fastest trip, etc).

The library and Internet are great resources for sailboat designs. If nothing else, a long straw with a short straw taped across it (forming an "X") will provide a good mast for a piece of plastic or cloth to act as a sail. You can form a hull by cutting a small milk carton in half (lengthwise, so that you have a natural keel). Fill your hull with some sand, and then put in your mast and sail. Instant sailboat!

PARENT-TO-PARENT ASIDE

Work can be tiring. When I finish the work week, I'm looking forward to catching up on my rest. I like to sleep in. But, if you have children, you have responsibilities. So, keep them busy. Interact. Go places. Convince them to join intramural sports teams. Is there a recreation center nearby? See when the sign-up periods are, then go to their games. My daughter tried cheerleading a year or two at these leagues. (I still have her tiny cheerleading outfit. Go Mustangs!) I can guarantee that boredom will not do you or your child any good, and they will get bored unless you keep them active. You'll grow tired, weary, and you might even be thankful when they're old enough to drive and can ferry themselves to events (even though you should still go), but try to catch up on your sleep later—after they've moved out and gone off to college or their own apartment or house.

WHILE YOU'RE DESIGNING AND BUILDING BOATS:

✳ Why do boats float? (The displacement principle.)

✳ What's the displacement principle? Is it because the weight of the water displaced by the hull of the boat (and air inside) weighs more than the boat? (And if it's heavier, it sinks?)

✳ What kind of boat did Christopher Columbus have? (Columbus' flagship was the *Santa Maria*, a sailing vessel with three masts.)

✳ Are you going to name your boats?

✳ See how many different kinds of boats/ships you can name. (For example, cabin cruiser, catamaran, sloop, aircraft carrier, speed boat, paddlewheel boat, canoe.)

CHAPTER 8

Holiday Fun

While I have included the holidays my household celebrates, you might celebrate different ones. Feel free to adapt the practices in this chapter to your own family traditions.

No matter what the holiday, these celebrations are times of the year when traditions are embraced and reinforced. It's a time for bonding with your children and for giving them a sense that no matter what problems a family faces, traditions go on. It's this sense of continuity that helps our children maintain healthy states of mind. It also gives them a notion of what we as parents value, such as on Thanksgiving, and the importance of being thankful for the good things in our lives.

It's important, too, to have a talk with your children about tolerance. Emphasize how important it is for your kids to practice tolerance to their classmates and other children who practice other religions. It seems that intolerance stunts the emotional growth of children (or anyone else!) and with a world that seems to be getting smaller daily, tolerance is vital for our own emotional well-being.

HOLIDAY FUN ACTIVITIES

New Year's Day • Valentine's Day

Easter • Memorial Day

Fourth of July • Labor Day

Halloween • Thanksgiving

Christmas • Birthday

NEW YEAR'S DAY

Make a tradition out of this—sit down at the table on New Year's morning and discuss what your resolutions for the new year will be—together. Encourage your children to have at least three resolutions each. Or, resolve to have no resolutions! (But come on, better grades are always a good resolution.)

PARENT-TO-PARENT ASIDE

Holidays can be a difficult issue when the parents are living apart, whether by divorce or another reason such as a temporary job relocation. Which parent gets the kids on Christmas Day? Christmas Eve? What about the Fourth of July? Halloween? While some divorces have holiday terms written into their papers, many do not. My personal policy has always been to be as flexible as possible—and to expect the same from my ex-wife. This has always worked out very well for me and my children. If you're a divorced parent, remember that your primary concern should be for the well-being of your children (not your ego or the destruction of your spouse's or ex-spouse's reputation as a parent).

WHILE YOU'RE CELEBRATING NEW YEAR'S DAY:

* Attend a New Year's Day parade.
* Ask your children to describe the best (and maybe the worst) moments of the previous year.
* Ask your children what they are going to do differently this year.

VALENTINE'S DAY

Help your children write Valentine cards to their friends. Depending on your children's artistic desires or the amount of time you have, you can make this a large project or a small one. Have construction paper (plain printer paper works, too), scissors, and markers available. Cut the paper so you get pieces that, when folded in half, they are big enough to write on. After folding the pieces in half (so that it opens like a Hallmark card), write the name of the recipient on the front. Then on the inside folds, you can add pictures, poems, anything! The main idea here is to get in a "Happy Valentine's Day" somewhere along the line. You can add the sender's name on the back.

Your children can be as creative as they would like. Encourage them to write poems, or draw hearts with arrows through them. If you have thick construction paper, you can cut cards into different shapes, such as circles. Another idea is to add pictures cut out from magazines or printed from the Internet.

> **FUN FACT:** *Each year, there are about 1 billion Valentine cards exchanged.*

PARENT-TO-PARENT ASIDE

This is a great time to talk to your children about different kinds of love. There are many different kinds of love for other people. You love your mother in a different way in which you love your spouse, but both fall under the category of "love." Also, point out that there will be many kids who feel left out on Valentine's Day if they don't have a lot of friends. Convince your children that it's important to be kind and to create Valentine cards for more people than just their friends.

WHILE YOU'RE CELEBRATING VALENTINE'S DAY:

* If your children could create their own national holiday, what would it be?

* Does this idea (arrow through heart) come from a portrayal of Cupid? What does it mean—an arrow through your heart? Wouldn't that hurt?

* Make up the words to your own Valentine's Day song, then have everybody sing it!

EASTER

There are many traditions that surround Easter, from dyeing hard-boiled eggs, to the Easter egg hunt. The tradition I started ran like this: I would make a list of nine clues on one piece of paper (three clues per child). The oldest would read the first clue, and try to find the hidden Easter treasure, which in this case was a collection of goodies such as marshmallow chicks and chocolate bunnies. All three children, though, got an equal share of the goodies. From oldest to youngest, my kids would read the next clue on the list and lead everyone to discover the treasures. For example, when my youngest was very young, I'd have a clue such as: "People put coats here." Answer: a closet. Easy, right? As your children get older, you can create clues that are more difficult. For example: *Grok!* Answer: I placed a gift certificate into my copy of *A Stranger in a Strange Land*.

PARENT-TO-PARENT ASIDE

As a divorced parent, I might not have my kids over on the exact date of any particular holiday. Of course, this can happen for married parents, as is the case for retail workers or traveling businessmen. In any event, I made it a tradition to celebrate my holidays on whichever day I choose. For the kids, it's great. They get to celebrate twice. You might consider establishing a tradition, though, of celebrating a holiday a specific amount of time, say one week, before or after the official date. You could also start a tradition of getting together with your kids and deciding when to celebrate.

ON EASTER:

* Talk about why Easter is celebrated. (Easter is the Christian holiday that celebrates the resurrection of Jesus, although the holiday has been somewhat secularized to become the day when the Easter Bunny comes.)

* Are eggs symbolic of re-birth? Why? (They are symbols of re-birth partly because from an egg: life springs out of a inert shell.)

* Talk about how spring brings warm weather to much of the country, and how trees begin to grow leaves again.

* Talk about dormancy. Do any of your children ever feel like going into a cave (like a bear) and sleeping through winter?

MEMORIAL DAY

Talk to your kids about the meaning of Memorial Day. It may help to go see a parade. Maybe you can combine this holiday with a field trip to a museum. For example, there are many museums that have battle dress and weaponry from centuries past. There are also many battlefields that can be visited. Once you're back at the house, have your children draw a picture as a tribute to fallen soldiers from past wars.

PARENT-TO-PARENT ASIDE

Talking about fallen soldiers can bring up the subject of death and getting killed in battle. There's no need for graphic detail here, but avoiding the subject can only fuel fear. Be honest and upfront with your children (depending on their ages, of course) and talk about it in the way you might read an account in a history book.

ON MEMORIAL DAY:

* See if your children can find and clip out any news stories about how parts of the country are celebrating Memorial Day.

* Tell your children to ask their teachers what they think of Memorial Day.

* Write a letter of encouragement to soldiers and find a way to get it to the troops.

FOURTH OF JULY

There are almost always Fourth of July celebrations going on somewhere. If you're having problems finding a parade or fireworks display, try looking in the newspaper or calling up local minor league baseball teams. Find a place to go. Eat hot dogs. Buy some sparklers.

I just have one rule with fireworks and sparklers—nothing gets lit unless I'm present. Teach your kids safety first!

PARENT-TO-PARENT ASIDE

It's always a good idea to discuss with your children what the plans are for upcoming holidays. I'm sure you've noticed that I've mentioned discussing things with your kids a lot—after all, communication is important. For divorced parents, remember that when major things change in your child's life, they are bound to be confused over what time is "yours" and what time is the other parent's. Don't let them make their own assumptions, as they may not be true and may result in their becoming upset when they find that out. Instead, tell them what the plans are by discussing potential activities with them. Get their input. Children need consistency. They need schedules and routine.

ON THE FOURTH OF JULY:

* Talk about why America celebrates the Fourth of July. (The signing of the Declaration of Independence.)

* Sing the national anthem. See if they know what, precisely, the term "star spangled banner" means. (At the time when the song was written, during a battle, the stars were scattered, or spangled, on the flag instead of being arranged in neat rows like they currently are.)

* Is it a good thing to feel patriotic? Does this mean that we never question the actions of our government? Why? (This should be an open debate. Try not to overshadow your kids' instincts. They have a right to their feelings and opinions.)

* Is there a Fourth of July in other countries? (Okay, that's a joke. Every country has a fourth of July, but the United States is the only one that has it as a national holiday. Venezuela is close, celebrating Independence Day on the fifth of July.)

* See if your children can say "the Fifth of May" in Spanish. Is this date celebrated in Mexico? Why? (Many people believe think Cinco de Mayo, the Fifth of May, is the equivalent of Independence Day, but it instead celebrates the victory of Mexico over French soldiers and renegade Mexican soldiers at Pueblo, Mexico.)

* Is there a similar holiday in Canada? (Canada Day is on July 1 and celebrates the formation of the Dominion of Canada, which formed from three British territories in 1867.)

LABOR DAY

Labor Day is usually a great weather day and usually near the start of the school year. Make the best of the last weekend (unofficially) of summer with the kids and go on a picnic. As a weekend parent and someone who works during the week, the time needed to accomplish household projects such as rebuilding the deck or painting the house sometimes falls onto my holidays. For Labor Day, though, it's a day that's meant to celebrate laborers, not a day to perform labor. So I've always made of a point of relaxing on Labor Day, and this usually meant a trip to the beach or a city pool. And because colder temperatures are just around the bend, the year's final outdoor swim usually occurs around Labor Day.

PARENT-TO-PARENT ASIDE

As Labor Day approaches, it's a good idea to get your kids mentally prepared for school. Try to get ahead of the game by having school supplies and any new school clothes purchased and set aside, so your children will feel prepared. The mental adjustment to heading back to school can be huge after a summer of fun on frolic, so it might not happen overnight. Build momentum by mentioning it one day, then talking about it in greater detail as the time for school approaches.

If Labor Day comes and your children have already started the school year, this is a good time to address and problems or anxieties that they're experiencing. It's also a good time to double check with them on any extra school supplies they might find handy.

WHILE YOU'RE CELEBRATING LABOR DAY:

* Ask your children if they know why leaves change color in fall. What is photosynthesis? Can they explain it? (Photosynthesis is the process plants and trees use to turn sunlight into food. The fall colors in trees were always there in the leaves, but masked by green chlorophyll. As chlorophyll production ends in the fall, the green goes away, exposing the other colors.)

* See if your children can get extra credit in school for learning about why leaves change color.

* Talk about how Labor Day came about. Is it a holiday for the workers (laborers) of the country? (Labor Day came into existence in the late 1800s as workers began organizing into trade unions and wanted more recognition for their efforts.)

HALLOWEEN

Halloween is one of my favorite holidays. Most families have their own traditions around this holiday, and I encourage you to create your own. Mine involve carving pumpkins and going trick-or-treating.

Carving pumpkins can be dangerous, so make sure you are prepared. When my children were young, I'd have them draw the faces on the pumpkins with a felt tip pen. Then I'd do the carving myself. It's interesting (in a Freudian kind of way) to see what kind of faces they choose. One of my sons likes horrific pumpkin faces. The other likes goofy ones (eyes uneven, mouth above nose). My daughter goes for the traditional smiley pumpkin face.

It can also be fun to plan for trick-or-treating weeks ahead of time by designing and creating costumes for the kids. If all else fails, you can use a simple sheet with eyehole cutouts for a ghost costume (but I suggest you urge your children to be more creative).

PARENT-TO-PARENT ASIDE

Unfortunately, it's a sad reality that there are dangerous people living in this world who would do children harm. It's therefore very important that you search your children's candy when they bring it home. Usually in the days before Halloween, local news stations and newspapers will talk about what to look for. This kind of information can also be found on the Internet, but local sources can be informative about problems that have occurred in the past in your particular area.

ON HALLOWEEN:

* Ask your children if they understand the difference between pretending to be a ghost and an actual ghost.

* Are their any safety alerts out for trick-or-treaters on the local news channels?

* Where does the term "trick or treat" come from? (It's an American phrase started in the 1930s and came from a good-

natured threat that if candy is not received, there'll be a trick played on you!)

* Have they ever tried pumpkin pie?
* Discuss planting a few pumpkin seeds next spring.

THANKSGIVING

I'm a Detroit-area native and my Thanksgiving tradition involves a game of football on the TV because the Detroit Lions pro football team traditionally plays on Thanksgiving Day. So I watch the game with a pile of turkey and dressing! *Yum yum.* Hey wait—this is about parenting activities. Thanksgiving is a great time of year to take your children to see relatives. Invite relatives to your apartment or house. Maybe you can make it a pot-luck affair. One thing, though, it's always fun to see who in the house can best make a sound like a turkey. (Tape recording is optional.) Another fun thing to do is to help your children rake leaves into a big pile so that you can all go jump on it.

PARENT-TO-PARENT ASIDE

This is a good time to bring up food. (No pun intended!) While turkey might be a traditional Thanksgiving offering, teach your children how to cook a special meal of their own. Experiment and make different dishes. Every child would love to be the owner of a "secret recipe." Maybe it'll be pumpkin pie with a special seasoning. If nothing else, a special kind of ice cream dessert is easy to do. Adding specific treats to a bowl of ice cream, such as strawberries and cake sprinkles, personalizes it and helps make your child feel special.

WHILE YOU'RE CELEBRATING THANKSGIVING:

* Talk about what your children are thankful for.

* Talk about the sacrifices people have made for our country and its citizens, such as military personnel and volunteers who help the needy.

* Talk about the history of Thanksgiving and the New England colonists. They must've certainly been thankful for the food the American Indians shared.

* Do your children know that Benjamin Franklin wanted the turkey to be our national bird? Okay, so the eagle won out. Probably a good decision from the founders of this country.

CHRISTMAS

FUN FACT:

According to some traditions, there are 12 days of Christmas because that's how long it took the 3 kings to arrive in Bethlehem after seeing the star appear in the sky.

I usually don't have our celebration of Christmas on Christmas Day. We normally end up opening presents a few days before or a few days after because my ex-wife likes to have the children on this holiday. What this means for the kids is that they get to have two present-opening celebrations. I usually take turns letting the kids hand out presents from under the Christmas tree. Then, all at once, everyone opens the present. We show it off, then another hand-out.

PARENT-TO-PARENT ASIDE

As I've already noted, the Christmas holiday season can be a very stressful time for both parents and children. Personally, I believe it's because expectations are so high. Everyone wants the holiday season to be perfect. Then, of course, after the holidays are over, there's an emotional letdown. Just a piece of advice: Don't get caught up in the holiday trap (at least not too much). My personal goal for the holiday season was simply for my children and I to spend some enjoyable time together unscathed and for the kids to get at least a couple of presents they liked.

For a lot of people, money is an issue. I personally didn't want to spend money on a Christmas tree, one that I'd be throwing away in a week or two, so my children and I worked on a compromise to get a "Christmas branch." We would take clippers and go outside to find an evergreen branch that we liked, clip the branch, and bring it home. It never held quite as many Christmas lights as a full-fledged tree, but the spirit was just the same. Other money-saving ideas include purchasing used toys from yard sales and secondhand stores, stocking up on gifts at bargain or dollar stores, and making gifts yourself. We've all heard about the Christmas when the best toy for a child was the box that the real toy came in. Sometimes for older children, something purchased second-hand for a few dollars can be priceless.

ON CHRISTMAS:

* Remind your children why Christmas is celebrated in the first place.

* Discuss how much fun it is to give gifts, as well as receive them. Do your children get a good feeling in their hearts by giving gifts? Ask them why it's called the season of giving.

* Talk about how Rudolf (the red-nosed reindeer) was an outcast among the other deer, but saved the day when Santa Claus couldn't find his way in the fog. Of course, then all the reindeer loved him. Talk about what it feels like to be a hero, and talk about some of your real-life heroes.

BIRTHDAY

Host a birthday party on or around your child's birthday. It's important to remember that even if there is a huge party planned for your child on the weekend, you should make an effort to give them a call or special note, or call them on their birthday day itself (especially if it falls during the week when you will not see them). When my children were ten or younger, I would also make sure that each child got a small gift, no matter whose birthday it actually was. It never had to be much, but it helped to instill the notion that everyone always shares—even birthdays. Of course, the birthday boy or girl should always get the most attention and gifts, but this practice made the others feel special, too.

PARENT-TO-PARENT ASIDE

There are many ways to get groups of children to come over for birthday parties. An activity that's highlighted in your invitations helps to bring everyone over, such as a bowling party (with bumpers up, of course!). Depending on the weather, simple outdoor games and the promise of a birthday cake can be a big draw. Make sure to find out if anyone has food allergies so you're sure the cake can be safely eaten by all.

ON A BIRTHDAY:

* What are your children's favorite holidays? What are their least favorites? Why?

* Have your children noticed that for many holidays, there's a theme of bringing families and family members together?

* Discuss the memorable birthdays that you've had and what they mean to you now.

* Search the Internet for famous people born on your children's birthday. (Mine is the same as Einstein's!) Your children might be fascinated by the company they share.

* Read a horoscope from the newspaper or Internet, especially if you find one that starts with "if today is your birthday."

* Explain that children's birthdays are special days for parents, too! Tell your children stories about the days they were born.

CHAPTER 9

Learning Things to Do

(While Growing Up)

At some point every child needs to be considered a young adult. They enter a period of "coming of age." It's reasonable to assume this age is different for different children. But how do you know it's time? It's difficult to pinpoint precisely. There used to be debutante parties, and in some families there is a ritualistic hunting trip with Dad, and the shooting of the first deer. Try to think of something that will help your child understand that you're beginning to think more and more that he/she is a young adult, with more responsibility. When I think back on my own history, it may have started when I gave my young son a homemade certificate for a free shaving lesson.

LEARNING THINGS TO DO ACTIVITIES

Sewing

Shaving

Tool Use

Card Designing

Magazine Subscriptions

List Making

SEWING

This is one of those tasks that your children will use throughout their lives. Teach them how to sew on a button after it comes off a shirt or jacket. Sew a patch on blue jeans. Sew on some embroidery or a cool dragon patch! Look for sewing projects online or at your local library. There are also sewing projects available at some of the larger retail stores and at most craft and hobby shops.

Of course, some young boys might consider sewing an activity just for girls. Nonsense! What if Sir Edmund Hillary popped a button on his parka on the way up Mount Everest? I'm sure he would know how to sew it on, otherwise he'd freeze!

PARENT-TO-PARENT ASIDE

When my daughter broke up with her first boyfriend, I offered to hurl insults and soap his car windows—not that I would have. (And I think she realized this.) But it sure made her feel better. There's nothing like sticking up for your kids. But I think my best advice to her—and this only works if she knows the relationship is truly over—is to imagine a voodoo doll in her mind, a voodoo doll that was the "relationship" and imagine doing whatever she wants with the doll. Try to find something that fits your style of parenting that works for you.

WHILE YOU'RE SEWING:

* Talk about how much money you save by sewing on a button compared to buying a new shirt.

* Where does the term "seamstress" come from? Is this a gender neutral term? (Because many pieces of clothing have seams.)

* Who was Betsy Ross and what did she sew? Could your children sew together an American flag? How would they do it? (Betsy Ross sewed the first Stars and Stripes American flag.)

* What other types of mending are there? (Gluing, welding, patching, etc.)

SHAVING

This is often a rite of passage for fathers and their sons. Shaving off that first chin hair can be a huge step on their way to adulthood. Make sure to purchase a razor that is theirs alone.

It may not occur to you, if you're the father, that you could teach your daughter how to shave her legs. It's possible she may not want your input, if you come out and say it directly. Try instead lending moral support, and guiding her by example. Show her how you shave her face and say, "Imagine my chin is your knee."

PARENT-TO-PARENT ASIDE

There are many topics about personal appearance that you will undoubtedly have with your children. It's good to be prepared early for their questions. For example, what if they ask you about tattoos? If you don't think they're a good idea, you might tell them that you have none and that they might give some employers a negative impression. It depends on the employer. Regardless of their questions, it's best to teach by example, and to relate it to your own life. Let your principles guide both you and your children.

WHEN YOU'RE SHAVING:

* Ask your children to name as many people with beards as possible.

* Do they know anyone with a mustache?

* Talk about Rip Van Winkle. (Rip Van Winkle is a character in a story by Washington Irving. Rip Van Winkle slept for 20 years straight and awoke to a world that had changed a great deal—and a very long beard!)

* Do beards, in general, make people look younger or older?

* Why does facial hair and leg hair mean that children are approaching adulthood?

> **FUN FACT:**
> *Abraham Lincoln was the first president in office to have a beard.*

TOOL USE

Even if everything in your home or apartment is in good working order, you should take the time to teach your children the basics on using tools, whether they are hammers, screwdrivers, or wrenches. You can do this in a couple of ways, from fixing up items at yard sales, to building things from scratch, like a hope chest, or hanging a picture on the wall. If you've bought those plastic toy tools for all those years for birthdays and Christmas, at some point it's going to be time to learn how to use the real thing!

PARENT-TO-PARENT ASIDE

In many manufacturing factories, you'll find signs and placards that read *Safety First*. They serve as reminders that no matter what the task, safety is the first consideration. You wouldn't use a power drill to make a hole in a piece of wood sitting on your lap because you think about safety and what will happen when the drill bit goes through the wood and possibly into your leg! Always consider what will happen if something slipped. There are many car mechanics with banged-up knuckles because they lost control of their wrenches. So, think *Safety First* and talk about it with your kids.

WHILE YOU'RE TEACHING HOW TO USE TOOLS:

* Explain the difference between the English system of measure and the metric system of measure.

* Are there different tools for the different measuring systems? Why? (Many tools have different scales, so a ruler can measure both inches and centimeters, which are units of length in different measuring systems.)

* Given unlimited resources, what would your children have in a tool kit?

* How do some people remember which way to turn a screw? (Rightie-tightie, lefty-loosie.)

* What are some other things that you routinely measure but are not length? (Instead of a ruler, you would use a pressure gauge to measure the pressure in your car tire.)

CARD DESIGNING

Almost every month, there's a new event that requires a greeting card. Instead of spending time visiting Hallmark, teach your kids to do these on the computer or to draw and design by hand! The older the kids, the more complicated this project can become. Pick up a book on origami, and try making a card out of folding paper. Getting your kids to make something (a birthday present or mom's or dad's day present) for the other parent (or, for a relative, or maybe even a friend), is a nice gesture and can be much more meaningful for the recipient. It's good to teach your kids that it's nice to give as well as receive, especially something homemade!

PARENT-TO-PARENT ASIDE

It's okay to tell your children that, on occasion, they need to cry it out. Yes, even boys. It's more than okay—it's healthy. Humans need periods of grieving. They need to work the hurts out of their system. If your child's relationship ends, don't say, "Don't cry." Tell 'em it's okay. Sometimes I wish I could cry more than I do. It's tough. Boys especially are told to "be a man" which means don't cry, don't show emotion. That's why we have so many adult men who aren't "in touch" with their emotions. Don't teach them to hide away their feelings. Come to that happy medium.

WHILE YOU'RE DESIGNING AND MAKING CARDS:

* Can your children remember the last time they got a card in the mail? Did they save it? Did it make them feel good?

* Ask your children what kind of card they would like to get in the mail.

* Do your children like humorous cards? Cards with poems on them? Cards with cartoons on them? Cards with flowers?

> **FUN FACT:**
> *Hallmark Cards, Inc. was founded in 1910, when the price of a postage stamp was one cent.*

MAGAZINE SUBSCRIPTIONS

Sit down with your kids and discuss subscribing to a magazine in your child's name. I've tried *Popular Science* and *Psychology Today,* but *Seventeen* and *Mad Magazine* are the ones that get read the most. This ties back to my comments about reading and learning: The important thing is that your children are reading. Having a magazine that's "theirs" also gives them a feeling of ownership and belonging at your place, and gives them something to look forward to when they come over.

PARENT-TO-PARENT ASIDE

As I've noted elsewhere in this book, reading is important for a child's development. Hopefully, you've earmarked this idea and your kids become active readers. As they grow older, keep an eye on what they're reading. It helps you to gauge their interests, which change as they get older. My son's interest in political satire has helped clue me in to his outlook in life. My daughter's subscription to *Seventeen* made me realize she was becoming a young woman.

WHILE ON THE SUBJECT OF MAGAZINES:

* Take your kids to the library and have them sample the magazine racks for ideas of what magazines are available.

* Find copies of magazines at yard sales and at your local library. (I've found copies of *National Geographic* for ten cents each.)

* Where does the term "periodical" come from? (It's a term for magazines that are published once each "period" of time. For example, *TV Digest* is a periodical that is published weekly.)

* If your children could design and produce their own magazine, what would they make? Why?

LIST MAKING

Not only is this book a list of 101 activities, "Make Lists" is one of them! Seriously, if you're going on a camping trip, or perhaps just off for a day at the beach, it's a good idea to have your children starting to learn how to make lists—and how important they can be. They might start to realize this when their underwater goggles are left at home because there was no list to check before driving off. Try getting into the habit of writing a list before starting any projects, from cooking to making a birdhouse. This can be great preparation for school (for example, "List the Great Lakes!").

FUN FACT:
A list of available food in a restaurant is called a menu.

Parent-to-Parent Aside

Nobody's perfect. There will be times when you forget something, whether it's an extra baby bottle on a trip to the mall, a towel to the gym, or to pick up milk from the grocery store. Sometimes your kids will be with you. It's a good time to bring up the advantages of being organized, of having lists, and the disadvantages of not thinking ahead!

While You're Making Lists:

* Talk about different ways of organizing a list. What are the many ways to organize? (Least to most expensive item? Largest to smallest item? Most to least important?)

* Come up with a to-do list.

* How many examples of lists can your children find around the house or apartment? (Lists of ingredients in the kitchen, songs on CDs, and more.)

* Are TV guides lists?

* What kind of list would be important to teachers? To people in the government? To the President of the United States?

* On what date of the year do many people make a list? (New Years Day—a list of resolutions.)

CHAPTER 10

Winter Activities

• •

If you live in an area that receives little or no snow every year, I suggest you do everything possible to save up enough for a ski/sledding trip, or perhaps a trip to a place where they can build snowmen and throw a snowball. Perhaps a relative's house?

Having fun in the snow is something your children will always remember. You can see the wonderment in their eyes as they watch their first snowfall. This gives way to excitement as you bundle up in preparation to go outside. It's such an adventure for younger children, even if you're going only as far as your own front yard. So when winter comes, grab those gloves and scarves and enjoy!

WINTER ACTIVITIES

Snowmen

Skiing

Sledding

Sculpting Snow

Snow Trekking

Snow Play

SNOWMEN

FUN FACT:
Sunlight reflecting off snow on the ground can cause sunburn.

Every child needs to have experience building a snowman. Snowmen are prevalent in our culture around the Christmas season, so whenever your children see one on TV, they'll relive the day they spent with you and built snowmen. Don't feel restrained to building just a snowman, however—you can make dogs, rabbits, or other animals. Be creative and encourage their creativity.

PARENT-TO-PARENT ASIDE

Statistics show that small children lose body heat faster than adults. Even if it seems like they're so active outside that they'll generate more than enough heat to keep them warm, it's important that they're dressed properly for the weather. Remember to have them wear multiple layers of clothing, which helps keep them warm. Consider waterproof boots or galoshes to keep their feet dry. Mittens generally keep hands warmer then gloves. Also, hats are imperative! Most body heat escapes the body from the neck up.

WHILE YOU'RE BUILDING A SNOWMAN:

* Ask your children why kids make snowmen and not snowwomen (at least, mostly they don't). Is this a gender neutral concept?

* Challenge your children to come up with interesting "make-up" for the snowman. Maybe a mop head for hair? Sure, carrots make great noses, but what else would work?

* Make one big weekend snowparent and smaller snowchildren surrounding the parent.

SKIING

I've taken my children skiing about four times in their lives. This might not sound like much, but they all know how to ski. I figure that when they're grown and taking care of themselves, they'll be able to decide for themselves if they want to ski more. At least they know how to ski. And when asked if they know how, they've always taken pride in the fact that they can, which is well worth the investment.

PARENT-TO-PARENT ASIDE

There's no doubt that skiing can be an expensive outing. There are ways to cut costs, though. Many organizations, like the Boy Scouts, Girl Scouts, and church youth groups offer group rates on day ski trips. If you can manage going during a weekday, it's usually less expensive then. Check newspapers and online to look for deals.

WHILE YOU'RE SKIING:

* Many ski resorts give free group lessons to young children. You should take advantage of this, but remember to hang out in the area to help your child if the going gets rough.

* Give them maps of the ski slopes. See how many slopes you can go down.

* Ask about the differences between snow skiing and water skiing. (Besides the obvious difference in required clothing, snow skis are much narrower than water skis. Instead of gravity to go downhill, water skiers have boats pull them.)

* Ask your children if there's anything else they should have brought to help stay warm.

* Make it a point to watch the next Winter Olympics together.

> **FUN FACT:**
> *In the Winter Olympics, contestants in the biathlon compete in both cross-country skiing and marksmanship.*

SLEDDING

The beauty of sledding is that it only takes a sled, a slope, and some snow to get started. I suggest finding a place near your home so you can always return to warm up if your hands or feet get too cold. If the snow isn't packed, you might need a toboggan instead of a sled.

PARENT-TO-PARENT ASIDE

It's odd how perspectives change as we grow older. I remember going sledding as a child. What do I remember? Racing down the hill, of course! But now when I watch children sledding, they spend most of their time trudging back uphill. Funny, I don't remember that part. Keep this in mind and give your kids those thrilling memories of sledding downhill, even if it means the long chore of walking back up.

WHILE YOU'RE SLEDDING:

* Ask your children what pulls you down the slope? (Gravity.)

* Is it friction that tends to slow you down? (Yes. Try going downhill on a sheet of cardboard, which has a rougher surface—more friction—and you'll go slower.)

* Ask if your children know about snowmobiles. Would they like to ride in one? (Maybe you can pretend you are as you sled down the slope.)

* Would waxing the bottom of your sled help? Why or why not? (Waxing the sled's rails reduces the friction and you'll go faster.)

SCULPTING SNOW

There are snow sculpture contests on TV that I see every winter. The sculptures are wonderfully varied. Castles. Mermaids. Reindeer. Sometimes the design is abstract, shapes and curves that simply look good. While you and your children might not aspire to such grand creations, snow sculpting can be a lot of fun. Build your sculptures in front of your home so that others can see the result of your craft.

PARENT-TO-PARENT ASIDE

When your children are younger, making a snowman is a great way to have fun. As they grow older, they need more challenging projects in order to grow. You want to help them discover their creativity. Snow sculpting is a perfect activity for this. It's like graduating from paint-by-number to drawing on a blank sheet of paper. And unlike the clay activity in this book, with snow you have so much more material to work with! Make a dog or cat four feet tall. How about a snow flower with petals as big as your hand? The sky's the limit!

WHILE YOU'RE MAKING SNOW SCULPTURES:

* See if there's anything you can add to the snow sculpture to give it more color. Maybe food dye?

* Have a contest for the biggest/most interesting/most original sculpture. Everyone in your family should win at least one category!

* Invite everyone in the neighborhood to contribute to a large community sculpture. Invite the local media to run a story on it.

FUN FACT: *It only happened once in recorded weather history—snow fell in the Sahara Desert in 1979 (although it melted within hours).*

SNOW TREKKING

This activity is similar to taking a hike in the summer, and yet it's quite different! Snow adds an entirely new dimension to walking overland. Hiking through snow, depending on its depth, can be almost as challenging as trying to run through knee-deep water at the beach. So pick a destination, bundle up, and set out for your hike through the snow. Maybe you can suggest wanting to get a picture with your camera of your children standing beside that big snow-covered tree in the field down the road. Maybe your goal is a picture of your church when it's draped with snow.

PARENT-TO-PARENT ASIDE

If you're walking through deep snow, your children will quickly learn that it's easier to walk behind someone else who is in the lead. The person in front is the one who has to trample the snow for everyone else behind. During your trek, walk single file and let everyone have a turn in front. An important aspect to this activity is having the hot chocolate (with tiny floating marshmallows) ready when you return home. After an adventure like trekking through snow, the warmth and closeness that sharing hot chocolate brings is . . . well, heartwarming!

WHILE YOU'RE TREKKING THROUGH SNOW:

* Talk about how difficult it must be for people in Alaska to get around during winter. Thank goodness for snowmobiles! They can be handier than cars in the far north.

* See if your children notice how sound carries better in cold weather. If not, point this out to them.

* Discuss the advantages and disadvantages of living in an igloo. (Having only one room is great to keep the warmth centrally located, but there's so little privacy!)

* See if you can find any animal tracks in the snow. Try to identify what made them.

SNOW PLAY

Most of the games that are generally played in warm weather can be loads of fun when played in the snow. Hide and seek is much more difficult when you have to consider hiding your footprints in the snow! How about a game of tag on a course made by trampling paths through the snow (make sure you have a safe zone). A game of soccer, with makeshift goals at the ends of your yard, takes on new dimensions with the addition of snow. Tag football can be fun for the older kids. Football and soccer fields can be marked in snow with a spray bottle filled with water and food coloring. If the weather's cold enough, you can make a "snow slide" by packing snow (use a snow shovel) into the shape of a slide, then watering it down and let it freeze. (Water it and let it freeze a second and third time to make sure it'll hold up.) Frozen snow slides can provide hours of winter fun!

FUN FACT:
It takes an average of 9 to 10 inches of snow to equal 1 inch of rain-water.

PARENT-TO-PARENT ASIDE

I try to keep my kids out of those tempting snowball fights. They've probably seen them on TV or at the movies, and they'll want to throw snowballs as a result. But it never fails that even if a snowball fight begins in good-natured fun, it ends with someone getting a snowball in the face, ending all of the fun that you've worked so hard to plan for. Provide alternatives to your kids. Find some targets, such as milk cartons, and explain that the best snowball-thrower is someone who can knock down the target with the fewest throws. Hitting a target at fifty paces should be enough of a goal.

WHILE YOU'RE PLAYING IN SNOW:

* Make sure you keep tabs on how cold they are. Sometimes those small fingers can get very cold, very quickly.

* Have hot chocolate ready once playtime is over.

* Ask your children if there's anybody they'd like to invite over to join in the fun!

* Standing on the sidelines is so much better than just heading inside, where you can't interact at all with your children while they play. But even better, try to join in the fun!

CHAPTER 11

Parenting from the Car Trunk

Let's say you arrive somewhere 10 minutes early. It could be at church, a movie theater, a bus stop, a school activity, or even the drop-off spot with the other parent. It could be for even more than 10 minutes. What are you going to do? Talk? Well, that's not a bad idea, but—depending on the age of the children—this can be intimidating. Your children might feel pressured to say something they don't actually mean, if they are having a bad day, or they may feel as if they are being interrogated. To solve this problem, I keep a cardboard box in my trunk with various toys. Children will enjoy the spontaneity (or they'll go along and make you think you're doing a good job). What follows is a list of what I keep in my trunk. Items have changed over the years, as my children grew older. You could start with these suggestions, and ask your children what else they'd like you to keep in your trunk. Have them write up a list and give it to you on your next parenting weekend.

ITEMS FOR THE CAR TRUNK
Frisbee • Golf Club
Notebooks and Color Pencils/Markers
Football • Cards • Books
Lacrosse Sticks

FRISBEE

Not everyone is a Frisbee disk-tossing tour de force. It doesn't matter. If you need a bit of practice before you impress the kids, try going out on your own and throw one against a wall. Soon you'll be able to show off in front of your children and make them want to be just like you! If you have more than one child, try standing in a circle and toss the Frisbee clockwise in a circle, or make a game of it and throw it at random, or see how many throws can be caught successively without a drop, or play a game of keep-away. If you have four or more people, try pairing off with a couple of Frisbees.

Because there's usually someone not quite as skilled as the others, it's important to keep an eye on who is being thrown the Frisbee so that one of the children isn't shown less attention.

PARENT-TO-PARENT ASIDE

There is a certain amount of joy in simply playing a game, regardless of the game's outcome. It can be downright fun! Beyond the "competition" aspect of the game, the goal of winning, there's also the pleasure of playing. The best thing I feel I accomplished with my children is I taught them a sense of joy. There are plenty of times for serious moments. Your children need to see you laugh: Go outside and wrestle. Tickle your kids! You need to have fun playing with your children.

WHILE YOU'RE THROWING FRISBEES:

* Select a tree (or some object that is fairly indestructible) and see how many tosses it takes to hit it. You could even lay out a course and play Frisbee golf. It's a hit on college campuses.

* Talk about the shape of the flying disk. What other shapes are similar? (Clay pigeons? Flying saucers from outer space?)

* See if you can make the Frisbee disk curve to where you're throwing it instead of going in a straight line. What other throwing object returns to your hand? (Boomerang.)

* See how many throws you can make with your children without the Frisbee disk touching the ground.

GOLF CLUB

I keep a putter in my car trunk, along with a few golf balls. Take turns trying to putt the ball into a "target," which can be anything from an empty Coke can to a rock. When first starting out, it's a good idea to have your children take a practice swing without the putter in hand. This is so that you have confidence they won't be taking wild swings. Make sure your kids understand that errant golf balls can do a lot of damage, not only to windows and cars, but to people as well.

FUN FACT: *In 1971, astronaut Alan B. Shepard Jr. hit a golf ball while standing on the moon.*

PARENT-TO-PARENT ASIDE

Let your kids attempt to do things. Trial and error is one of the best learning methods. Let them try stuff out, and allow them the luxury of failing without a parent getting visibly upset with their failures. That can be very upsetting to them as well, and may cause them to grow up inhibited by feeling they need to do things perfectly the first time. By allowing them to try (and fail), they may learn that there is lots of stuff out there in the adult/real world that they might be good at, and that most things need practice.

WHILE YOU'RE TEACHING GOLF:

* See if your children can come up with any theories as to why golf balls have dimples. (They fly farther and with more accuracy in flight.)

* What did Mark Twain mean when he called the game of golf "a good walk spoiled"? (Golf courses are usually scenic—great for a nature walk—but playing the game gets in the way.)

* Where did the game of golf originate and why was it banned in 1457? (Scotland. The king banned golf because it interfered with archery practice, which was necessary for defense of the realm.)

* Ask your children if they enjoy golf enough to try out for a school team when they're older. (As with anything else, they'll have to practice.)

NOTEBOOKS AND COLOR PENCILS/MARKERS

When you're sitting in the car, you can pull out a drawing pad and sketch. Take inspiration from the surroundings, or perhaps even each other. You might try a game of hangman. How about asking them to draw their favorite cartoon characters? For younger children, drawing shapes can be fun. How about drawing a car, perhaps different kinds of cars, like SUVs and compacts, or even a motorcycle? Take a look at the drawing suggestions in the "At Home" chapter on page 18. Remember to have your kids compare their pictures.

PARENT-TO-PARENT ASIDE

When showing you their pictures, your children will be hoping for praise for their work. Go ahead and give it. You might want to point out a thing or two they could do differently, and that's ok. I've noticed that children can sometimes be fairly harsh with each other when evaluating each other's drawings. This brings to mind my general rule of thumb regarding art criticism, and perhaps criticism in general. Always point out something that was done well, and since nothing's perfect, point out what could be improved, and always give two suggestions for how to achieve the improvement.

WHILE YOU'RE DRAWING NATURE SCENES:

* Ask your children if there's a difference of perspective in each of the drawings. (For example, a prominent NBA player commented once at how odd it was that his children always drew grownups with legs three times the length of their torsos. When he knelt down to their eye level, though, he could see that from their prospective, the drawings were accurate!)

* Is anyone better at drawing a still scene as opposed to a live animal? Vice versa? Have the children vote on each other's pictures.

* Have everyone draw a picture of the box in the trunk with all the parenting items!

FOOTBALL

If you're stranded at a park or a parking lot, get out the old pigskin and play catch. Go out for passes, or even simulate passing plays that you have seen on sports highlight clips. Hut! Hut! Hut!

If your children are still young, try using a Nerf football instead of a leather football. It's easier for them to catch and much safer if they are just learning.

Football can be a rough sport, even if you're only playing flag or two-handed tag football. This doesn't mean that daughters don't want to play! You'll want to make rules to even the playing field, such as making any contact (such as blocking or grabbing) a penalty. So, make sure everyone understands the rules, then go out and have fun!

> **FUN FACT:**
> *The first football used in a game was round.*

PARENT-TO-PARENT ASIDE

A lot of the items in my trunk kit are sports related. I'll be the first to say that I spend too much time in front of a TV, but I do try to get outside for anywhere from a half hour to an hour per day. Most kids in this day and age watch too much TV, play too many video games, and don't have enough physical activity. So, when there's an opportunity to spend some time outside playing catch with a football or Frisbee disk, it's a good idea to take it.

WHILE YOU'RE PLAYING CATCH WITH A FOOTBALL:

* Talk about the local high school football team. Does anyone know anybody on it?

* Ask your children if they have any aspirations in sports.

* Did they know that many athletes receive sports scholarships to colleges?

* Talk about the Olympics. Try to name as many Olympic events as you can. Can they name any events in the decathlon? (100-meters, 400-meters, 1500-meters, 110-meter high hurdles, javelin, discus, shot put, pole vault, high jump, and long jump.)

CARDS

The great thing about cards is that you can carry a deck around in your pocket (and there should be plenty of room in the car trunk). Check out the cards suggestions in the "At Home" chapter, page 13. While in the car, though, you might have a problem finding a flat surface, making some card games difficult.

You might try the game of War. Deal out all the cards evenly. Everybody shows the top card in their pile. The high card holder wins all the cards and puts them in the bottom of his stack of cards. Repeat this process until somebody wins all the cards. If you want to quit before then, whoever has the most cards wins.

In the game of Pig, everyone passes a card to someone else. Keep the card if you want and pass a different card. Continue to repeat this process. The first person with four-of-a-kind touches his or her nose, signaling winning the game of Pig. You can find other card games online or in books at your local library.

PARENT-TO-PARENT ASIDE

There will always be sibling rivalry. There will always be a decision that has to be made and one of your children won't like it. Who gets the last piece of candy in a bag? Who gets to go first on a carnival ride? These are good opportunities to explain that as a parent you don't particularly enjoy making these decisions. You don't want one of children to have more than an equal opportunity to succeed (or go on a carnival ride) than one of your other children.

I've noticed that children have an inner detector of fairness, even if it's just perceived fairness. It's important that your children know that you're trying to be fair. Your children will emulate you when they grow up. If you want your children to have a sense of fair play when they grow up, treat them fairly as children. This gets me to my point—sometimes there's no true way to determine who gets to ride the roller coaster first. I suggest taking the deck of cards, shuffle them, and have each child pick a card. Highest card wins the day. This should come with the understanding that the next time this situation arises, the other child gets to go first (or gets the last piece of candy).

WHILE YOU'RE PLAYING CARDS:

* Have your children see how many differences they can find between the jacks, between the queens, and between the kings. (For example, two of the jacks show one eye instead of two.)

* Ask your children if they would like to invite their friends over for a game of cards.

* If they want to play cards while you're driving, be careful not to be distracted.

* See if they can think of different ways of shuffling the cards.

BOOKS

Books are always a good idea to have in the car. I keep several books in the passenger section of my car, and magazines, too, especially ones like *National Geographic*. I prefer to keep things educational but fun (and *National Geographic* has really cool pictures!). For the trunk, I suggest packing a book on nature as well as a book that identifies trees by bark and leaves (color and shape). Or, maybe one that identifies plants. If you're coming up long on time, take your kids on a nature walk and try to name the trees.

PARENT-TO-PARENT ASIDE

This is a good time to mention poison ivy. For deeply urban settings, this might not be an issue, but the adage "Leaves of three, let it be" would have saved me a breakout or two in my younger days. It's not just poison ivy that is dangerous, however: there's also poison sumac and poison oak. Make sure your kids know what these three look like and to stay away!

WHILE YOU'RE IDENTIFYING TREES:

* Why do some trees have large leaves and some small? Do small trees have smaller leaves? Is this always the case? (The size of leaves for different trees evolved from their environments in part to capture the most sunlight. Some small trees, like the Pawpaw tree, have very large leaves.)

* If trees are competing for areas to catch the most sunlight, what would give them an advantage? (Taller trunks. Larger leaves!)

* Why are there so many streets across America that have names such as Elm Street and Maple Avenue? (Partly tradition. Originally, a street lined with many maple trees could be easily identified as Maple Street.)

* Where does the expression "as strong as an oak tree" come from? (Oak wood is very strong.)

THE PRACTICAL GUIDE TO WEEKEND PARENTING

✳ Do palm trees have a survival advantage in areas of Florida frequented by hurricanes? What is it? (Palm trees have strong trunks able to bend without breaking and leaves that do not present a large area for wind to push against.)

LACROSSE STICKS

Lacrosse is an up-and-coming sport in the USA. Get a head start and teach your kids to be the first kids on your block to learn how to play catch with lacrosse sticks! Your kids will think it's so cool to be able to do something that no one else can do. Search online for tips on how to carry a lacrosse ball. The ball is "cradled" in the lacrosse stick's netting by twisting your wrist up and down. You can set up a target, such as a bucket or pail, and try to shoot the ball in. Lacrosse balls are very hard, so use caution! When starting out, you might want to try using a tennis ball first. No matter what kind of ball you use, you'll want to have lots of extras when starting out so you can just pick up an extra instead of searching for the one that just went into the woods.

PARENT-TO-PARENT ASIDE

Depending on the ages of your children, they will probably be at different levels of maturity. Their skills will vary. It will be difficult to have your children play lacrosse (or perhaps any other sport) if one is thirteen years old and the other five. If at all possible, take the older or more skilled child aside and explain how that child was young at one time, too. And that it's important, as a family, to play together. As long as nobody tries anything more than a simple game of catch, everything should work out fine. You could, for example, also have the older child only pass "slow grounders" to the younger child.

WHILE YOU'RE PLAYING LACROSSE:

* Who invented the game? (American Indians. They played on fields that were miles in length.)

* What other sports are played with pieces of wood, such as hockey, baseball, and last but not least, the javelin throw? (Actually, for the Olympics, the javelin can be made of either wood or steel.)

THE PRACTICAL GUIDE TO WEEKEND PARENTING

* Why are sports games played with a set of rules? What would happen if there were no rules? (Let your children answer this for themselves.)

* What kind of rules are there in life? Laws? Codes of conduct? Why makes an activity "wrong"? Is it just because it might be illegal? (You may want to guide your children with these answers, but be careful not to preach!)

CHAPTER 12

Quick— The Kids Are Here!

You haven't planned to have the children over. Maybe you forgot. Maybe there's been a sudden change in plans (such as a snow day at school). Perhaps you've been busy all week and don't have a thing planned—or perhaps your funds are running low and you want to stay at home and keep everything under budget. Whatever the reason, there are times when your children come over and you haven't done any advance planning. The activities in this chapter are for those times.

QUICK ACTIVITIES

Cooking Meals • Puzzles

Video Games • Cartoons

Carve Out New Space • Home Repairs

Bake Cookies • Design Your Own T-Shirt • Charades

Weather Investigation • Finger Painting

Mobiles and Dreamcatchers

COOKING MEALS

My parents never had me cook a meal, and I never really showed an interest in learning how to cook. Still, there were two things I did prepare: Omelets and French fries. While it didn't work for me, it's not a bad idea to have your children learn to prepare meals, at least in some cursory manner. Even if you are as inexperienced of a cook as I, there are cookbooks galore, and perhaps you and your children can learn together. You will probably need to view the recipe before a trip to the supermarket. (Work those list-creating skills!) Let them try to bake a cake, and pick out the frosting! If all else fails, start very simple and make cookies using the pre-made cookie dough.

PARENT-TO-PARENT ASIDE

Don't worry about doing any of these activities perfectly, especially the first time out. If you start a scrapbook, just get that first item onto the first page. It's a start. That's all you need to do at first—get a start. You'll gain momentum later. If your cake doesn't rise or your boat design project turns out boats that don't even float—laugh it off! The important thing is you're spending time with your children. You are teaching by example, so if you are demanding perfection from yourself while saying to your kids "It's okay if you don't do it perfectly the first time," they will focus in on what you are doing instead of what you are saying. Be sure to practice what you preach.

WHILE YOU'RE COOKING MEALS:

* Talk about nutrition. What are vitamins? Nutrients? Why does it matter what we eat? (Our bodies need proper nutrition for good health.)

* Talk about the phrase, "An apple a day keeps the doctor away." Who said that? (Benjamin Franklin.)

* What does having a "sweet tooth" mean? (You have a fondness for sweets.)

* Do your children know that acclaimed chefs can make excellent salaries?

* If water has no calories, why do we need to drink it in order to stay alive? (To maintain health—the average adult body is 50–65% water!)

* See if anyone's interested in trying a new food, something your children have never tried before. Anyone for Lima beans? How about mangos?

PUZZLES

Patience required! There are many puzzles for different ages, from simple to very complicated. You will also find 3-D puzzles that are available. I suggest creating a workspace so you won't have to disturb the puzzle between weekends. I like to get a large piece of cardboard, start assembling the puzzle, and then slide the cardboard (with puzzle) under the sofa during the week until its completed. You can buy puzzle glue to hold the pieces together when you're done and place it in a frame and hang it on a wall.

PARENT-TO-PARENT ASIDE

It's a good idea to let your children do most of the work. Stay involved, of course. Maybe have them give you direction on what they'd like you to do, perhaps to work on a particular corner of the puzzle. Resist the temptation to help so that the puzzle can be put together more quickly. Patience is a good attribute when working with puzzles. Sometimes it's painstaking work and it can be difficult to sit and watch your children struggling to find the right pieces. But that makes the payoff all that much greater!

WHILE YOU'RE WORKING ON A PUZZLE:

* Talk about why patience can be a very good attribute to have.

* Is there a different puzzle your children would like to get?

* Ask if they'd like to make their own jigsaw puzzles by drawing pictures on sheets of paper, then cutting them into pieces.

VIDEO GAMES

I remember when we got our first Playstation console. Mario was a big hit. However, as my children grew older, my daughter dropped out of the video gaming arena and my boys moved on to shoot 'em up games. They are now, at least, trying out some strategy games, like *Sim City,* and the one where you plan out an amusement park. I suggest guiding your kids to more educational or thinking-style games instead of the first-person shooters, simply because it makes them exercise their brains (while having fun).

It's been my personal experience that the violence in these games has had no bearing on their demeanors or activities. But then, I'm an active weekend parent who talks to them and reinforces that the games are make-believe. Make sure you are one as well!

PARENT-TO-PARENT ASIDE

There's been talk of using "tough love" to raise children. Personally, I believe the best thing to do is to not cave in when you know you're doing the right thing. But, if I tell my son he can't do something, and then later I realize that I hadn't thought it through and that there really shouldn't be a problem with his doing it, I cave in. "Okay," I tell him (after listening to his arguments), "go ahead." Make sure there's a little flexibility with the tough line.

WHILE YOU'RE PLAYING A VIDEO GAME:

* Talk about how a car (or Mario Brothers cart) crashing in a video game is different from a car crashing in the real world.

* Are they any video games where there's no winner? A cooperative game? What about *The Sims*? What's the point if there's no winner? (Prompt them to come up with their own answers.)

* If your children could design their own video games, what would they be?

* Ask them if any of their friends talk about video games. If so, what do they say?

> **FUN FACT:**
> *Atari launched the home video game revolution with* PONG *in 1972.*

CARTOONS

It's nice to keep up with the culture your children are living in. Of course, you can tell (every fall) from the designs on backpacks and school notebooks about what's popular. One year the "in" thing could be the Ninja Turtles, and the next it could be Spiderman. Watching cartoons with your kids will give you an opportunity to laugh with them and comment on a TV show that they want to watch. You'll begin to know their world, from which characters like SpongeBob SquarePants infiltrate our adult pop culture.

PARENT-TO-PARENT ASIDE

It's nice to have a spirit of cooperation in the household. Sometimes that's easier said than done. Here's one way to help instill a "you scratch my back and I'll scratch yours" frame of mind. Let's say your child has a chore that needs to be done, whether it's homework, a chore, or mowing the yard, but for some reason or another doesn't want to do it. So your kid, knowing you have an "open door" policy, asks you for help. Even if you're busy, it's a good idea to at least put in some effort to help. This is when you point out that there might be times when you're the one who needs help. Siblings can pitch in, too, and you can make the same point, that doing favors will end up in getting favors.

WHILE YOU'RE WATCHING CARTOONS:

* Ask who your children's favorite cartoon characters are. What makes them the favorites?

* Talk about some of the older cartoons you watched when you were a child.

* Why do they have so many commercials? Is the food shown during commercials on Saturday morning display healthy food? Can toy commercials be a source of greed?

* Show them cartoon strips from your local newspaper.

CARVE OUT NEW SPACE

One thing I learned as my children grew older—they get bigger! The older the kids got, the more stuff they began to bring over on the weekends. It could be CD players, computer game systems, or even schoolbooks, but at some point, your kids will begin to need more space. In the beginning, I had at least one shelf and one dresser drawer for each. Later, I got each a small dresser. At some point, it's nice to have a conference with your children and talk about their space needs. Then, go shopping together, whether it is at a yard sale or to a store for something new. You could also make this a home improvement project and build items from scratch.

PARENT-TO-PARENT ASIDE

Kids need to be responsible for keeping their own space neat, even if they are only there once or twice a week. Don't fall into the trap of allowing them to be messy all weekend, and then leave you with the sweeping, vacuuming, and picking-up of toys after they have left. While it's a great thing for your kids to look forward to weekends with you, it shouldn't be because they can "goof-off" and avoid all their responsibilities while at your place. Make sure they know they are responsible for keeping their space neat, and picking up well before it's time to go.

WHILE YOU'RE CARVING OUT SPACE:

* Find some pictures and show your children how much they've grown (but try not to embarrass them with naked-kid-in-tub photos!).

* What size house or apartment would your children like to have when they grow up?

* What does the term "I need my space" mean? (It's human nature to want an area that you have control over.)

* Do your children get uncomfortable if someone is too close when talking to them? Why does space give a level of comfort? (It's cultural. In different countries, the "comfort zone" varies.)

> **FUN FACT:**
> There's a chest of drawers in the city of High Point, NC that is four stories tall!

HOME REPAIRS

Let's say the leg on your coffee table is wobbly. Or perhaps there's a fixture in your bathroom that's leaky. Enlist the help of your children. It'll give them a sense of accomplishment and teach them basic skills that will come in handy in years to come. Figure out the tools and supplies that you will need, and take a trip to the hardware or department store. Once you make the repair, make sure to go on a celebratory lunch or ice-cream cone trip!

PARENT-TO-PARENT ASIDE

Your kids may still be too young to help, but intensely interested in what you are doing. So, if they're very young, have them use their plastic toy tools and pretend to help. Make a big deal out of it. I realize that often they're more in the way than actually helping, but the point of this isn't to accomplish the repair as efficiently as possible, it's to involve your children in the day-to-day activities at your house.

WHILE YOU'RE WORKING ON HOME REPAIRS:

* Ask about what the term "handyman" means. Is this a gender neutral term? (Let them answer without prompting.)

* Can girls be just as good as boys at fixing things? (Of course they can!)

* Talk about the importance of maintenance. (It's much cheaper to keep something in good repair, spending a bit of money here and there, than waiting for it to break beyond repair and spending a lot on a replacement.)

* What are the causes of things breaking? (Wear and tear, abuse, improper maintenance, etc.)

* How did the pyramids of Egypt survive for so long? (The Egyptians learned to build pyramids that were sturdy; also, the limestone blocks they used were capable of surviving the effects of weather.)

BAKE COOKIES

If you're rained out, or need a quick afternoon activity, break out the cookie sheet and bowls and bake some cookies! It's a good idea to introduce your children, especially when they are young, to the ideas behind measuring spoons. It may be their first introduction to science. And two parts this, one part that sounds an awful lot like math. If you don't prefer cookies, bake a cake! You don't need to make either from scratch if you're not keen on cooking, but it's definitely much more of a learning experience.

PARENT-TO-PARENT ASIDE

Baking is a wonderful way to show your children how math and science are not only practical, but they can be fun, too! It's so easy for kids to think that math is something that's only done at school or during homework. The more you can get your kids to practice math with fun projects, the better. Think about a lemonade stand. Children have to plan for the amount of lemonade they need, the cost of supplies, and what to charge in order to make a profit. For younger children, try games with flash cards. Check online and at your local library for other fun projects that use math.

WHILE YOU'RE BAKING COOKIES:

* Can any of your children remember a commercial on television that advertised cookies?

* Why bake cookies when you can just buy them? (It's not as fun and many don't taste as good as home-baked.)

* Why is being self-sufficient important? (There will be times in life when there's no one else around to help.)

* Who's the Cookie Monster? Is the Cookie Monster really a monster? (This Sesame Street creation is a monster, but a relatively good-natured one.)

* Try to guess what the favorite cookies of famous people are, and why they are their favorites? (I imagine John Wayne didn't like oatmeal cookies. Too mushy.)

DESIGN YOUR OWN T-SHIRT

With a tiny bit of preparation, which you are able to do even after the kids have arrived, you'll be able to entertain them for a few hours and send them home with a souvenir. Head to a department store or craft store and buy a pack of white t-shirts and permanent fabric markers. There are dozens of colors available. Sit with your kids and plan a design on paper first, then help them draw it on the shirt in pencil. Have each fill in the designs with fabric markers. Why not design a family logo?

PARENT-TO-PARENT ASIDE

Some children have no problem joining in with the fun. Others can be reluctant, sitting on the sidelines, and let the more active kids do everything. Although you don't want to push too hard, you want to help draw quiet children out of their shells. Give them more one-on-one time and be patient. Let them join in a little at a time. And remember to praise every effort, and that it's the effort you're showing an appreciation of, not the result of the activity.

WHILE YOU'RE MAKING T-SHIRT LOGOS:

*   Ask what kind of logos your children see on clothes of classmates. Tommy Hilfiger? Nike? What about sports teams logos?

*   Is a simple design better than a complex logo? What are the benefits of each? (Simple logos are easier to remember but convey less information.)

*   Does your children's school have a logo? What about a team mascot? Do they think it's a good mascot?

CHARADES

I never tried playing charades until we had an extended power outage due to an ice storm. I was amazed at how much my kids enjoyed playing. The games also spurred their imagination—always a good thing. This is a great evening or afternoon activity that really makes your kids think. So, maybe start a charades league. Find children (and maybe parents, too) in the neighborhood and form teams. Then have each team play each other team in your league twice. Charades is also a great game to play when you are waiting in the car.

PARENT-TO-PARENT ASIDE

There's nothing wrong with you (or your kids) being silly. You and your kids just have to know when it's time to stop. This time comes when your kids begin to get out of hand and begin to stop listening when you ask them to take it easy. You can usually tell if your children are getting tired, frustrated, or hungry, and this might indicate a good stopping point in playtime. Having a snack or taking a shower or bath can be a good post-game activity for cooling down.

WHEN YOU'RE PLAYING CHARADES:

* Talk about signals and gestures that we use in everyday life, such as the thumbs-up sign, crossing your fingers, and holding your hand out, palm forward.

* Talk about how some games can be fun and exercise your mind at the same time.

* Talk about mimes. Mention the famous mime Marcel Marceau, who was the only person who said a word in the Mel Brooks film *Silent Movie*. Ask if they'd like to see a mime performance.

* See if you can get one of your children to bring you a glass of water using only hand signals.

> **FUN FACT:**
> *King Louis XIV in 1654 played charades, giving clues to proverbs by dancing ballet.*

WEATHER INVESTIGATION

If it's raining outside, or perhaps it looks like rain, take your kids on a weather investigation. Spend some time looking up folklore predictions on the Internet or at the library. Write them down, and have your children try to predict the weather based on cloud formations. Here are a few I can think of:

* Red sky at night, sailors' delight. Red sky in morning, sailors take warning.

* Evening red and morning gray will set the traveler on his way; but evening gray and morning red will bring down rain upon his head.

* Rain before seven, clear by eleven.

* When dew is on the grass, no rain will come to pass.

PARENT-TO-PARENT ASIDE

Weather-related disasters, such as the effects from Hurricane Katrina, seem to be in the news a lot. These are good times to get with your kids and volunteer to help. Watch your local news and read the newspaper to find out specific ways you can lend a hand. For example, areas prone to flooding might need help making sandbags. Your children could make donations from their piggy banks or help with food drives. This helps them to understand how the act of giving can be a deeply rewarding experience. These are also good times to talk to your kids about childhood anxieties that might arise from news about disasters. One way you can help is to put together an emergency kit. Also, have flashlights handy in case the power goes out. It'll put your children at ease to see that you're prepared.

WHILE YOU'RE IN THE WEATHER MODE:

* Talk about why sayings may have been more important in an earlier era. Why are many of the sayings dealing with sailors? (Sailors needed to predict weather to avoid stormy seas!)

* Talk about navigating by the stars. Why is the North Pole so important?

* Which side would you want the North Pole on your ship if you were sailing west (say, like Columbus, from Spain to America)? (The right side, known to sailors as "starboard." Left is "port.")

* Buy a copy of the *Poor Farmer's Almanac*. Check to see how accurate the predictions in it are.

* How accurate can the weather forecasters predict six months ahead? Why is this so difficult? (Not accurate at all. There are far too many variables to do any mathematical weather modeling.)

FINGER PAINTING

While at first you may think this seems like an activity only for younger children, it can still be great fun for older kids. One of my favorite pieces of art from my children is their teenage handprints (different color for each child) on a blank piece of white construction paper, framed and hung on the wall. It's a piece of irreplaceable art. Older children might have fun trying to draw more complex pictures. Or perhaps they can imagine being a superhero that needs to develop fingertip sensitivity to develop those super powers. The "feel" of the paint is half the fun! Most other times we paint, we try to avoid getting paint on ourselves. Finger painting is like giving your children the freedom to make a mess. How can they resist?

PARENT-TO-PARENT ASIDE

You'll want to keep a close eye on your children for this activity. It's easy for finger painting to become wall painting. Having a bowl of water and towels ready nearby can help contain this activity to your finger painting area. An old plastic tablecloth can help, too. Check the type of finger paint and make sure it can be cleaned easily if there are any "accidents."

WHILE YOU'RE FINGER PAINTING:

* Talk about the difference between finger painting and painting with brushes. Which is more fun?

* What's a fingerprint? Why do people use fingerprints as a means of identification?

* Can your children see differences in their fingerprints? Compare theirs to yours.

MOBILES AND DREAMCATCHERS

To make a dreamcatcher, you need to find a very pliable twig or stick, one you can bend into a near-circle (actually, tear-shaped) and tie off. Think of what the pattern of a snowshoe looks like. Thin metal coat hangers work well. Local crafts stores are a good source for dreamcatcher sticks. Then take twine, or yarn of various colors, and tie one end to the stick. Loop the twine across the open circle to tie to the other side. Make crisscross patterns. Dreamcatchers were made by American Indians to capture nightmares before they could affect their sleep. They can be decorated with feathers, beads, and other objects. Mobiles are fun to make, too. Take your children to a store, or check online, and see what kind of mobile looks like the most fun to make. You can make a mobile with different hand-drawn fish, frogs, planets, fruit, butterflies, anything! You'll need string or yarn, glue, construction paper, crayons or markers, and a sense of balance!

> **FUN FACT:**
> *Dreamcatchers were initially made by the American Indian Chippewa tribe.*

PARENT-TO-PARENT ASIDE

I learned the expression "cool beans" from my children. I like it, so I use it occasionally. I think using the language my kids speak helps them understand that I am actually listening to what they're telling me. Although it's possible to overdo, try learning a few words and expressions that your kids use a lot. You don't want to appear like you're having a mid-life crisis, but it never hurts to make an attempt to fit in with your children's friends.

WHILE YOU'RE MAKING A MOBILE:

* Talk about the difference in materials needed for an indoor mobile versus an outdoor mobile. (Outdoor materials should be weatherproof.)

* Are mobiles a form of art? Have your children ever made mobiles in school?

* Why are mobiles with planets—a solar system—so popular? (The planets' orbits are a natural fit for how mobiles are constructed.)

CHAPTER 13

Advance Planning Required

● ●

Many of the activities in this chapter will take place over multiple weekends, or at least they can. By having an activity that requires multiple weekends, you can instill a sense of continuity in your children. That's good! Also, it'll give them something to look forward to from week to week. If they don't want to finish a particular activity, remember that they need to learn to finish long-term projects, too. This helps children understand that sometimes progress toward a goal can appear minimal at best. But by sticking with the program, they'll learn that some things just need longer to achieve. It'll make their sense of accomplishment that much deeper.

ADVANCE PLANNING ACTIVITIES

Movie Making • Rockets

Book Making • Collage

Acting • Scrapbook

Photo Album • Gold-Star Bulletin Board

Home/Apartment Redecorating • Volunteering

Boy Scouts/Girl Scouts • Musical Instruments

Bridges • Ant Farms

MOVIE MAKING

We're entering the digital age. Actually, as my children point out, most everyone else entered it long ago. Whether you're using a digital camera or VHS tapes, wouldn't it be great to play producer and director—and make your own 20 or 30 minute movie? You could even send out copies as Christmas presents! This worked great for me and actually saved a lot of money because the copying isn't expensive at all.

Sit down with your children and decide what kind of movie you want to make. A western? A science-fiction thriller? (This was our choice.) Or maybe a drama. How about action/adventure? Maybe something like a soap opera. Write down the scenes, the dialogue, and talk over the action of the storyline. In ours, aliens invaded earth and it was up to my children to save the planet (which, of course, they did). You can work on costumes, scene settings and props, and "choreograph" the movements of the actors.

PARENT-TO-PARENT ASIDE

If you are parenting on the weekends, don't make the mistake of realizing that you can't also make phone calls during the week. (Or even graduate to emails.) It's good to keep in touch, and keep up a casual dialogue, even if it's just a "Hey! How did school go today?" Let them know what you're doing. Ask them about projects they have for school. Ask if they're having any problems. This lets them know you're always there to support their efforts.

WHILE YOU'RE MAKING A MOVIE:

* Talk about your favorite movies. Why are they your favorites?
* What's the worst movie you've ever seen? Could it have been made better? How?
* If you had the best movie studio in the world and unlimited resources, what movie would you make?

ROCKETS

While going to the nearest Toys 'R Us and buying one of those pre-packaged rockets won't take the entire weekend, you can easily stretch this activity out with "prep" time. Spend some time at home on the Internet or the library researching what kind of rocket you and the kids want to get. What are their goals for the project? (Maybe they want to build one with a capsule so that they can send insects soaring into the sky.)

PARENT-TO-PARENT ASIDE

The activities in this book are designed to be fun. Sometimes, though, activities that require a lot of time could cause children to become uninterested. If their attention flags, try to rejuvenate it by throwing a "let's finish this project!" party. Turn on some music, bring in some snacks, and make a good time of it. Tell them you understand their frustration, but to trust you. The payoff at finishing the activity will be worth the effort.

WHILE YOU'RE AT ROCKETRY:

* Does your rocket use solid propellant? (Most hobby rockets use a solid propellant because these are safer than other propellants.)

* What fuel does the space shuttle use? (The shuttle's main external tanks hold liquid hydrogen and liquid oxygen for fuel.)

* How do fins help a rocket to go straight? (They guide the rocket much like a shark's dorsal fin keeps the shark going straight.)

* What force tends to make your rocket return to earth? (Gravity.)

> **FUN FACT:**
> The first man-made satellite was launched in 1957 by the Soviet Union and was named Sputnik (the Russian word for satellite).

BOOK MAKING

FUN FACT:
A "double-decker" is a book published in two volumes.

No matter what the age ranges of your children, you are able to help them with a long-term project like a book. If they are in the younger ranges, try making a picture book. (You know, a simple story like a talking fish that makes friends with a shark.) Or they could use crayons and construction paper. Once they are older, you can still make an illustrated story; simply leave spaces for the illustrations after writing out the story in a notebook or on the computer. Printer paper works well if you prefer not to have lined pages; otherwise, simple notebook paper will work. Once the book is finished, you can copy, staple, and send these out as Christmas presents to distant relatives. Spend some time giving the story a title.

PARENT-TO-PARENT ASIDE

When your child comes to you with a problem—this could be anything, from a problem at school or even with a classmate—I ask "What would you do if you had a magic wand?" Our children need to learn how to solve problems but sometimes can't imagine the solution. Of course, this may net you answers like "make the bully go away" which might not provide a practical solution. However, this will at a minimum help pin-point what exactly is the source of the problem. Sometimes that's all you need to know in order to suggest a solution.

WHILE YOU'RE WRITING AND ILLUSTRATING A BOOK:

* Talk about the importance of reading.

* How many authors can your children name?

* Look at some editorial cartoons in the local newspaper. Can you get any ideas from these?

* How about making a comic book? Are there moral lessons derived from comic superheroes?

COLLAGE

Take a large picture album, a notebook with thick pages, or a poster board. This will be the base of a new project with a thematic (and artistic!) statement. Tell your kids that their goals are to find things that work towards that theme. They can find the objects anywhere! You can cut out pictures of magazines or use non-pictures like words from a newspaper, or even glue macaroni painted in different colors. For example, on one page, you could print at the top: "Work toward success." On the next: "Caring for friends." There are endless possibilities. How about: "I love my weekend parent."

PARENT-TO-PARENT ASIDE

I haven't been a hands-on disciplinarian for my kids. I did spank them when they were young and there were issues of safety and the child didn't respond to a verbal no—especially when they reached toward electrical outlets. NO! Still, there's such a thing as political capital. There's only so much of your ability to say no. It's fine to lay down rules (and in fact children need these so that they know the boundaries), but as different situations arise, pick your battles. Don't say "no" as a knee-jerk reaction. Save your "no's" for when it matters the most.

WHILE YOU'RE WORKING ON A COLLAGE:

* Talk about your theme and why it's important to you.
* Ask your children what each thinks would be a good project for classmates.
* What is a "theme"?

ACTING

Pretend you have a stage. You can make up your own play, or do a performance of *Grease,* for example (abbreviated, of course). You might have to make up a few props, school bus seats, for example, if your play is going to be about what goes on during the ride to school each day. If they're very young, they can do a "sock puppet" play. Regardless of the format, they'll have to write down what the actors in your play are going to say—the script. It's a good idea, depending on the age of your children, to take them to a play before tackling this activity. They can get ideas on stage props, dramatic speeches, actor interaction, and all of the other aspects that make a play entertaining. If you take your kids to a play, be sure to talk to them about what was interesting to them, and what wasn't. This conversation might get them to start thinking about what they would do different. Also, remember that most successful plays build up to the ending. Ask your children, as they develop the script, how to make the ending of your play memorable!

PARENT-TO-PARENT ASIDE

I have one daughter and two sons. I've often wondered about whether or not I treat them differently. I might be tempted to say that I've been more protective of my daughter—you only have to look at the reports of child abductions on TV to understand my concern. But in today's world, I have to say I've been fairly protective of my sons, too. One thing I will say: all three were unique and different from birth. One was gregarious and always wanted to socialize. One was always trying to be athletic. One was the observer. (You have to watch out for those quiet ones!) These traits have remained with them as they grew toward adulthood. Don't expect your kids to be what *you* want—help them to develop their own identities.

WHILE YOU'RE ACTING:

* Talk about how actors can cry when they're not really sad.
* Talk about the difference between reality and acting. Have your children ever seen someone pretending to be angry?

* Do infants ever "fake cry" in order to get attention?

* Have your children ever noticed anyone who's acting uninterested in someone else when they had a "crush" on that person?

* Why is acting considered to be entertainment?

SCRAPBOOK

Scrapbooking can be a project for years. You can put in movie ticket stubs, snapshots, class photos, Valentine's Day cards, or even articles from the newspaper that caught your attention. Talk to your kids about how nice it will be to reminisce years from now and talk about everything you did together. Announcements of achievements in school can go in. Anything and everything. This will also prove useful as your children grow up and near college age. Many application forms for scholarships have places where you need to put down extracurricular activity. You can look through the scrapbook and find activities your children participated in but might've forgotten. For example, I found it difficult to remember how many years my son participated in the local fall basketball league, and paging through the scrapbooks made it easy (and fun) to tally those years. He was able to include this information in his essay application to an exclusive high school for gifted teens.

Parent-to-Parent Aside

When your children are younger, they'll be much more apt to take your suggestions about trying particular sports, even if they aren't necessarily enthusiastic about it. As they get older, they'll discover what interests them most. You can continue spending time driving to soccer practices, but there's little point if your child's heart isn't in it. When do you let your children decide? It varied for all my children, and sometimes you have to come out and ask directly. By the time they reach high school, they'll probably know what sports they want to play, if any. Again, guide your children, don't force them. One of my sons opted for advanced musical training after school rather than a sport.

Some Other Items to Put in the Scrapbook:

* Mention in the local paper.
* Any group activity (such as boy or girl scouts) that gets mentioned.

* Any museum guide from a museum you visited.
* If you, say, go to the beach—put in a brochure that describes that beach.
* Photos.
* Short essays.
* Ticket stubs.
* Cards (birthday, etc.).

PHOTO ALBUM

Buy a small album from a dollar store if you're not ambitious at the beginning of this activity. Get a one-time use camera. Don't forget when budgeting that there'll be development costs, too. Because of these, I tend to only take few pictures at specific events—maybe only one or two, for example, at a play that one of my children is performing in. With a digital camera, you can take as many as you like and only print out the best. Collect the pictures in a shoe box (or on your computer until you are ready to get them developed), and eventually you can put the ones you like in an album. It's nice to have one photo album per child. You could have a separate one for the family album.

PARENT-TO-PARENT ASIDE

There comes a time when you might not particularly approve of the kids that your children are playing with (or, if they're older, "hanging out" with). Maybe these other kids aren't polite. Maybe they're mean or dishonest. Maybe they aren't smart. Maybe they're spoiled little brats. (Of course, our children never are!) This is a very tricky thing, because at a certain age, if you approach this too aggressively, your children will rebel and gravitate towards the ones you are warning them away from. When your kids are still young, I suggest going into "passive resistance mode." I don't actively discourage hanging out with the problem kids, but I might start keeping my kids very busy so they won't have time to hang out with the undesirables, and stop arranging play dates with them. I might also mention a thing or two (in general) about rudeness (and let your child realize the connection). It's so much better to have your children come to realize the truth by themselves without having you as a parent imposing a decree.

WHILE YOU'RE WORKING ON A PHOTO ALBUM:

* What are your children's favorite pictures?

* If your children could go anywhere in the world and take a picture, where would they go?

* What ways are there to organize the photo album? (Chronologically? By area of interest? By the season of the year?)

GOLD-STAR BULLETIN BOARD

Make a gold-star bulletin board. (This can be a poster board.) On the left side, write your children's names. Then, with each "achievement," you can put a gold star beside the name(s) and maybe write a short note that explains the achievement. For example, "joined chess club," "helped the clean house," or "has read 10 books." I placed my board on the wall where my children would see it as soon as they entered my house. This particular board didn't last long; about eighteen months, if I remember correctly. Still, it's something my children remember fondly. This also gives you a neat tool of positive reinforcement.

FUN FACT:
Gold is a metal but does not tarnish or rust.

PARENT-TO-PARENT ASIDE

Don't be overly critical. Most times, in school or in a sporting event or in an activity, your child knows if he/she screwed up. Just say, "Good job, I'm proud of you." You'll be amazed how far this takes you at being successful in weekend parenting. One of my sons missed an important free throw late in a basketball game. He was very disappointed in himself. Luckily, I was keeping statistics in a small notebook I would bring to games, and I could cite all of the good things he'd done in that game. Although he was still disappointed, it made him feel better, and deep down he knew I was right, that he had played well overall.

WHILE YOU'RE PUTTING UP STARS:

* Is there anything that deserves a double-star?

* What can you do to deserve your own weekend parent star?

* Should a star be given for thinking good thoughts? If not, why not?

* What do your children think is deserving of a star?

* Should you give a reward for a certain number of stars reached? (Possibly an allowance?)

HOME/APARTMENT REDECORATING

If you're a weekend parent, the chances are that you might've moved suddenly into a house or apartment and décor was, as a practical matter alone, the last thing on your mind. Involve your kids in your decorating. What sort of shades or furnishings or wall hangings (etc) do your kids suggest might look good in your new pad? Have them make suggestions. Would they suggest a rearrangement of furniture? Show them how to sketch out a floor plan on grid paper (where 1 square can be 1 foot). Get out a tape measure. Check the lengths of your furniture.

PARENT-TO-PARENT ASIDE

It helps to have positive reinforcement. Instead of just punishing bad behavior, give them rewards for good behavior. I think of it as a form of allowance. But instead of earning money for washing dishes, they earn money for consistently good behavior. But this isn't a weekly payout from me. I expect good behavior, period. It's just that sometimes I'll buy them a treat for it. Hopefully, they'll realize there are other benefits of good behavior. It's your job to get them to behave, then they'll see the light (especially if you hound them and point out the benefits).

WHILE YOU'RE REDECORATING:

* Is there a kind of theme (there's that word again!) that would look better but is less practical?

* If your children had unlimited resources, how would they redecorate?

* What kind of home or apartment would your children like to have? Why?

VOLUNTEERING

There are a lot of church and social organizations that need lots of help on particular days or at particular times of the year. For example, Habitat for Humanity. Spend some time volunteering for a few days (or even a month) and have you and your children help out. Call around and get suggestions to find a local group around you. There might be ways that you can help that you haven't thought of yet. How about the United Way? What about a soup kitchen? Go shopping and donate items to a food bank.

PARENT-TO-PARENT ASIDE

When my nephew was visiting (age 5), he just adored my daughter (age 17). One day, she and her boyfriend were doing the dishes. My nephew wanted to help. Sure, I said, just as soon as you go pick up and put away all your toys. Bingo. Toys were neatly put away lickety-split. Now, he really didn't help all that much with the dishes, but we managed to make him think he was a tremendous help—and he thought he had "earned" the privilege of helping!

PLACES TO VOLUNTEER:

* Schools. (Ask the principle how you can help.)
* Hospitals.
* Homeless shelters.
* Habitat for Humanity.
* AmeriCorps.
* Senior citizen housing. (You can volunteer to just visit with the residents or perhaps read to them.)
* Churches.
* Boy Scouts.
* Relay for Life.
* Call your local community's government for more local ways to volunteer.

BOY SCOUTS/GIRL SCOUTS

Joining the Boy Scouts or the Girl Scouts is a great idea to get your kid involved with other children their age, especially if you recently moved into a new area. The scoutmasters tend to be responsible adults who enjoy helping children mature into responsible, productive adults. You could volunteer yourself! If your children balk at entering the scouts, make a deal that they try it for six months, and then they can "resign" without any repercussions from you if they don't like it by then.

PARENT-TO-PARENT ASIDE

It's difficult to get kids to try something they don't want anything to do with. Brussel sprouts, for example. It's good to point out that it's very difficult to legitimately criticize something they haven't tried. Of course, they might counter with they've never jumped off a bridge, but that doesn't appeal to them either. Just remember that while guiding your children to adulthood, you want to reward good behavior, and show that bad behavior has consequences. So, if they don't want to try the brussel sprouts—just a bite, not a whole serving—then that means no dessert, or no trip to the Dairy Queen.

WHILE YOU'RE SIGNING THEM UP:

* Talk to the people who are running your particular scouting troop. Make sure you have a good feel for how they operate.

* Get contact phone numbers and email addresses.

* Ask about opportunities for summer camp and camping trips. (This can be a great way to bond with your kids on a budget!)

MUSICAL INSTRUMENTS

You don't need to have real instruments to get a band together. Teach your kids to make music out of the common household objects you have around. You can use coffee cans for drums. Fill up glasses with varying amounts of water, tap them with spoons for a xylophone. Use pan lids for cymbals. Make sounds by blowing across the tops of bottles filled with varying amounts of water. Try looking online or in the library for more ideas. Once you have all your instruments ready, invite your kids to bring friends into the mix and have a concert!

FUN FACT:
The invention of the brass instrument sousaphone was assisted by conductor John Philip Sousa.

PARENT-TO-PARENT ASIDE

Young kids need naps! (This can double as quiet time.) If kids don't get enough sleep, they get cranky, and no one likes it when kids are cranky. If they need to cry themselves to sleep, well, that's fine. Just go in every five minutes or so and check up on them. The trick is to appear to be NOT abandoning them; you're just not going to put up with childish behavior. By the way, I've noticed that my children don't like being called childish. Fair enough. But they certainly have to agree that some behaviors don't show a level of maturity that other behaviors show.

WHILE YOU'RE MAKING MUSICAL INSTRUMENTS:

* Ask if anyone at school ever talks about music.

* What are your children's favorite kinds of music? How about their favorite instrument?

* What's the difference between "noise" and "music"? Has anyone ever thought he/she was making music but it sounded more like noise?

* How many percussion instruments are there? Can your children name some? (Drums? Bongos? Cymbals?)

* What about stringed instruments? (Guitars? Violins? Harps? Banjos?)

BRIDGES

This is an inexpensive project that turns into a game of skill. Buy lots of popsicle sticks and glue (available in the craft section of a department store), work on a design, then go ahead and build one between two stacks of books. Then, collect some pennies and see whose bridge can withstand the weight of the most pennies. Give the winning child all those pennies! You can also build cabins and other cool stuff. How about picture frames (remember to paint)?

PARENT-TO-PARENT ASIDE

Competition can be brutal. I try to make sure that all my children win in different categories of my "events." There are some parents and psychologists out there who suggest that having "winners" and "losers" isn't a good idea because the losers will also lose some self-esteem. I agree that self-esteem is important for children. Children tend to go through stages in which they will disparage themselves. (Like when my daughter was convinced she was the ugliest girl in the world because of a lack of a boyfriend.) Still, I would argue that it's also important for children to learn to lose (and win) gracefully, to understand that there'll always be another day to compete. After all, they'll be in competition their entire lives—competing for jobs, scholarship money, even for a low interest rate on their house loans. Some days you win, some days you lose. It's all part of the process we call life.

WHILE YOU'RE BRIDGE BUILDING:

* Discuss why it's important to design sturdy bridges.
* Have your children ever seen traffic jams with large, heavy trucks idled and not moving atop highway overpasses? Did the engineers design their bridges with this possibility in mind?
* Talk about the metaphor of a bridge. If a bridge connects two land masses, what kinds of bridges connect people? (Religion? Love? Acts of kindness?)

ANT FARMS

Other than goldfish, the only pets I had for my weekend parenting were two gerbils (over 10 years). They made good pets—except they tended to get a bit smelly if neglected. Their names were Critter-1 and Critter-2. I let my kids decide; I only made suggestions. Of course, I kept veto power (as I do with all decisions), but I try to wield a veto only rarely.

Building an ant farm allows you to maintain a pet without having to do a lot of work. And if you're a busy parent—as most are—then an ant farm is convenient. Most toy stores carry inexpensive kits to start this project.

> **FUN FACT:**
> *Ants can lift 20 times their body weight.*

PARENT-TO-PARENT ASIDE

What is a human soul? See what your children think about this issue. My ex-wife and I have (and always have had) different views and beliefs about religion. We've used this as a tool to teach tolerance and the advantages of keeping an open mind.

WHILE YOU'RE TALKING ABOUT YOUR PET ANTS (OR GOLDFISH OR GERBILS):

* Talk about how animals should (or should not) be treated ethically. Where does hamburger and bacon come from? Why is torturing an animal wrong?

* Do animals feel pain? What about plants?

* Do some religions in the world believe in karma and reincarnation? In their religion, can souls come back and inhabit animals? Is that why cows are sacred in India?

Afterword

Parenting is tough work. Weekend parenting is just as tough as the day-to-day parent, and it presents different challenges. The weekends aren't your "time off" any longer. They become the days during which you get your opportunities to bond with your children and be a hands-on parent. It's my hope that this book helps weekend parents be better parents, and helps them to raise their children to be responsible, productive, fulfilled adults.

I hope that when you talk to your children, you begin to think of them as small adults (without very much experience in the world). Sooner than you think, they will be real adults, and the sooner they (and you) get used to this idea, the better it is for all. If you find yourself "telling" your children things, or commanding them to do this, ordering them to do that, and compelling them to think a certain way, you're going to find there'll be a rebellion at some point. Let your children make their own decisions (for the most part, safety issues aside) and live with them. But, guide their thinking. Isn't that what a parent is—a guide to adulthood?

If you have any questions or would like to talk about an issue, or if you have an idea you'd like to see in my next parenting book, I'd love to hear from you. Feel free to email me at: weekendparent@yahoo.com

I'm always looking for good parenting ideas, even if mine are now (mostly) out of the house, and I'll do my best to offer you the best advice I can—after all, I'm sure it'll be sooner than I think that I become a "weekend grandparent."

Happy parenting!
Doug Hewitt

Index of Activities